Republican

The ~~U S~~ ^ Constitution

N. L. Brisson

…this is a view from the cheap seats

The Republican Constitution

Table of Contents

Introduction

While it has been true until now that the US Constitution gave us the tools we need to legislate through our differences, and around them, and over them, we have reached a time when a major party has simply refused to use those legislative tools and has instead used the tools of obstruction. Not really a part of our Constitution at all, although the filibuster came shortly after ratification, these procedures arose out of use and have become part of the legislative arsenal. Arsenal is a good word to use here because since President Obama was elected these tools have become weapons wielded by Republicans to block the Obama agenda.

Republicans apparently feel that our Constitution has become too liberal and they want to adopt a more Fundamentalist (Conservative) view of the document. As a result, even our Constitution has come to be viewed through the lenses of partisan politics. Although Democrats may find that our body of Constitutional Law has become a bit too complex and that some tweaking is needed, the party on the left has not expressed major dissatisfaction with the Constitution. Republicans, on the other hand, seem to want to reinterpret everything about our Constitution (or they may just be exploiting it to win all three branches of the US government and pretending that their motives are idealistic).

It is unlikely that our forefathers would want a Constitution that serves slightly less than half of America's citizens, but the Republicans seem perfectly comfortable to own a sort of 'divine right' to reforming governance. The Evangelicals and Catholics, both against Roe v Wade and legal abortions for religious/moral reasons, have found that their interests coincide on more than just this one issue and their mandate on this matter comes right from God.

Both groups espouse Conservative ideas and together as a single demographic they form a fairly formidable group. They have made it clear in their media offerings that they believe when our forefathers argued for freedom of religion they were not thinking about religions that were not Christian ones. They feel little compunction about implying that Muslims are not covered by our Constitution and that atheists are not either.

Catholics and Evangelicals wish to ignore everything that happened since the birth control pill was first made available to women. They feel that we have angered God and messed with the natural order of things (was there ever a natural order of things?) and that since we have used contraception and abortion to stop births (kill babies) America's morals have slipped, as have our families and our fortunes. These devout folks obviously feel that we will prosper once more if we stop breaking God's laws. I have heard them argue that the separation of church and state is not stated in our Constitution. Others feel that if we are free to worship as we please that indicates that government cannot make laws about religion and cannot obey the laws of any particular religion. This is something the right wing seems to want to reexamine.

http://www.theocracywatch.org/separation_church_state2.htm

They have recently been enlightening us about what our forefathers actually meant by the First Amendment and the Second Amendment. They even managed to gut the Voting Rights Act before they lost their tenuous majority in the Supreme Court with the untimely loss of Justice Scalia. They have invented artificial intelligence far more lifelike than any coder has by getting the Supreme Court to rule that corporations are people and that they therefore have free speech, just in time for the Koch brothers and their cronies to buy the Presidential election in 2016 (at least until Donald Trump became the Republican candidate).

Is our Constitution as resilient as our ancestors hoped it would be? Can it survive this extreme right wing onslaught and still manage to serve Americans across the entire political spectrum? Can our founding documents be skewed to serve the needs of one political party only? Can the Constitution become a partisan document?

This book will examine the Conservative program during the Obama years as it affects the US Constitution. However I doubt that there will be a definitive answer at this time as to the outcome of the "coup" attempt on our nation and on our founding document. We may find out the answers depending on who wins the 2016 election. If a Democrat wins the Presidency the Republicans will have to wait and obstruct for 4-8 more years to implement their policies. If Republicans get their wish and all their maneuverings put them in charge of the Executive, Legislative, and Judicial branches of US government we could get our answers fairly soon. Will we like the answers we get? I say we will not. Others say we will be very happy with the end result.

Chapter 1

Sedition

Since I have been paying close attention to politics in Washington – since the first time I got a stomach ache listening to Glenn Beck in 2008 – I noticed that the Republicans have been tinkering with the U.S. Constitution. Certain sections of the Constitution were left deliberately vague by our Founding Fathers who were probably trying to create a document that would allow our fledgling government to evolve. It has worked for the last 200+ years.

However, I am worried that the ways in which Conservatives have tweaked the Constitution and have tried to prove they have a direct line to the forefathers has robbed the Constitution, making it look as if it supports the right as opposed to giving all viewpoints a voice. These folks have crept behind the curtain and made us question whether, once so exposed, our Constitution will ever again be a powerful enough force in American governance to get us through another 200 years.

At least four areas of the Constitution have suffered most from the biased attentions of the right wing. Conservatives have had very strong opinions about the section of the Constitution that discusses the rights that belong to the federal government and the rights that belong to the states. They also, as you may already know, pay particular attention to the First Amendment, the Second Amendment, and certain Supreme Court decisions like Roe v Wade and the Voter Rights Act.

Thinking Back

In the days of the American Revolution our forefathers were breaking away from their status as a colony of Great Britain and they were intent on designing a government that would correct all of the problems the colonies had with the "mother" country. The subtle and not so subtle controls exercised from across a rather large ocean were constraining and downright maddening to those who had relocated to the American colonies. Each colony wanted the protection of a centralized government and yet the autonomy of its own domain. The colonists, who were forced to give quarters (housing) to British troops in their own homes recognized that this robbed colonists of their freedom to defy the British. The British acted as spies who saw everything that the colonists did. Thus we see the roots of the Second Amendment, the right to keep and bear arms.

We all know the story of the taxes that the British levied on goods the colonists wanted to buy, especially the taxes on tea. Apparently there was a real yen for tea in colonial America. The colonists hated the idea that they had no say in deciding about what should be taxed, how much an item should be taxed, and who would get to use the tax revenues generated. We can assume that the taxes did not accrue to the colonial governments that had to collect them. The sections of the Constitution that cover the three divisions of our government, the executive, the legislative, and the judicial were intended to operate as a system of checks and balances so that no one colony (state) (party) would have an outsized influence.

Parts of our Constitution were added later or even much later than those added in early post-colonial times as in our Bill of Rights. They were added in Amendments, by executive order, or as part of the body of laws passed by Congress, and also by the Supreme Court in the form of disputed laws in which one side was upheld all or in part by the Court. Recently, for example, the Voting Rights Act, now 50 years old was challenged by the Conservatives and parts of the law were deemed no longer necessary by the Supremes.

This change in the Voting Rights Act is a GOP tweak which promises to have some negative effects on the minority vote in the 2016 election. Previously in states that practiced discrimination against minorities, especially Americans of African Descent, changes in voting were subject to review before they could be put in place. This is no longer true and a longer and more detailed look will show why some of these changes seem to prove that racism is alive and well in some parts of these United States, or, at the very least, that the Republicans are trying to suppress votes that traditionally go to Democrats (or both).

The Obstructionist 113th Congress

In 2013 Huffington Post gave us the following information about the educational background of members of the 113th Congress:

Education
• Roll Call Member profiles at the beginning of the 113th Congress, reported 21 members of the House and 1 Senator have no educational degree beyond a high school diploma.

• 7 Members of the House have associate's degrees as their highest degree, and 1 House Member has an L.P.N. (nursing) degree.

• 85 members of the House and 14 Senators earned a master's degree as their highest education degree.

• 169 Members of the House (38% of the House) and 57 Senators (57% of the Senate), held law degrees.

• 19 House Representatives have doctoral (Ph.D. or D.Phil.) degrees.

• 22 Members of the House and 3 Senators have a medical degree.

• 3 Representatives and one Senator in the 113th Congress are graduates of the U.S. Military Academy and 1 Senator and 1 Representative graduated from the U.S. Naval Academy.

• 1 Senator and 2 Representatives were Rhodes Scholars, 2 Representatives were Fulbright Scholars, 2 Representatives were Marshall Scholars, and 1 Representative was a Truman Scholar.

http://www.huffingtonpost.com/bill-lucey/113th-congress-by-the-num_b_2737382.html

Clearly there are a lot of lawyers in Congress. Perhaps this is why the Senate, in the hands of Republicans, has been finding ways to circumvent the intent of the Constitution using the wiggle room deliberately left in the document by our forefathers.

The GOP has not been in the mood to compromise with Democrats. They have been in the mood to stage a bloodless coup to get their way or to stop Democrats from governing until the Republican Party once again controls the Executive Branch. They have decided to be all checks and no balance but in order to do this they have had to convince the American people that they were trying to interpret the Constitution the way our forefathers wrote it. They made people believe that they were employing a more fundamentalist and pure form, a form that denies the 200 years of tradition and law that have defined the Constitution as we actually use it in the 21st century.

States' Rights and the Federal Courts Get the Fundamentalist Treatment

Republicans are using a State's Rights argument to turn the Constitution back in time even though we can only know our forefather's true intentions through the things they wrote and only through those writings which have survived. Perhaps Republicans have learned to travel through time, although we know they have not. Even our illustrious ancestors however would not be happy to see the Supreme Court politicized as it has been recently. The courts were supposed to be nonpartisan, but anyone can see that it is possible to pack the Federal District Courts and even the Supreme Court with people who hold beliefs similar to your party.

Once Republicans realized the power of having sympathetic judges, and once they realized that keeping a majority in Congress allowed the party to control who got on the courts even when they did not control the Executive Branch we were faced with the deadlock that we currently see in Congress. Republicans decided to keep control of Congress even if they had to undermine the spirit of the Constitution. Democrats say "do your job". Republicans say "it is our job to keep our courts out of the hand of the liberals" and to their people they justify this by claiming "the Democrats are ruining America". Their message, issued in a tight economy, has fallen on fertile ground. (I do not mean to neglect the role of racism in this. Their actions coincided with the election of our first African American President which made Republican opposition even more determined.)

Right Wing Strategies

Conservatives are organized. They talk to each other. They hold meetings, conventions, forums, etc. where they thrash out policy and practice speaking. They preach to the choir so to speak. They cheer each other on and rev up the rhetoric. In their newest incarnation they have talking points, a playbook which they all subscribe to and can generate some passion about. Conservatives have long mined American discontent on Talk Radio. They whipped up believers until they had a big enough cohort all over America to justify an entire channel on TV that could broadcast right wing talk pretty much 24/7. Fox News was been very successful at taking the Conservative message mainstream. People all over our nation listen to Fox News all day long and into the night. Covered in flags and patriotic lingo, mixing truth and lies and conspiracy theories, Fox News has brainwashed many Americans until they sound like Republican "pod" people whose bodies look normal but whose minds are occupied by aliens. This is hardly what our Constitution or our forefathers intended with all that freedom on their minds.

Almost every policy the Republicans have advocated is designed to somehow put them back in the White House and in control of Congress with the courts packed with sympathetic judges. The steps in their game plan include the Citizen's United decision, extreme gerrymandering, voter suppression, suppressing minority votes, blocking any amnesty for immigrants which would produce even more minority votes, pushing their agenda in the state legislatures through ALEC, winning control of state governorships and state legislatures, meddling in local elections by spending inordinate amounts on local elections, signing a pledge that promised no tax increases and using primaries to enforce the pledge, using similar threats to make sure the NRA gets what it wants, turning our courts into partisan bodies, playing to anger and fear and white privilege, discovering similarities between what Evangelicals want and what Catholics want, attacking women, attacking minorities, shutting down government.

What Republicans Want

What do they hope to do to America should they succeed? It seems that a lot of their plans are about the economy. Since they don't believe that climate change is real they want to restore the oil/coal based economy to its former glory but this time America will control the price of fossil fuels. Since this looks undoable they may have to rethink this. People do not seem ready to accept fracking everywhere or leaky pipelines meandering across their fresh water sheds. Perhaps Donald Trump's imperialistic plan to seize and hold Middle Eastern oil wells while that area of the world continues in disarray will start wielding more and more sway over the right.

The GOP would like to bring the factories back to America. They feel that when the factories left the world felt that this signaled a decline in the position of America as the top dog in the world. They want us to be the steel producers, the cotton producers. They want an America economy that is smoking along producing the world's goods once again. They pretend that if we keep the tax rates on the wealthy and on big business low that the benefits will eventually shower down on we the people and we will be back on the fast track once again. This is the trickle-down theory that is key to their economics.

In addition to low taxes on the rich Republicans want to have a balanced budget and to get rid of both our debt and our deficit. Not all economists believe that this is necessary or possible. In order to do this the Conservatives are preparing the American people to live without the government programs which back up those of us who are not wealthy, so that we can weather hard times. Programs like welfare, WIC, and food stamps will be the first to go. Medicare and Social Security will soon follow.

The GOP wants the federal government to cut the schools loose. Schools would either be private or paid for by the individual states. National standards for education would no longer pertain. Each state would decide on its own standards. They try to tempt citizens to go for this plan by offering vouchers which would allow kids to attend any school the parents picked for them. If you believe this will happen, that your child will be able to attend a school of your choice, then you have not lived in America for very long. However it would certainly be easier to balance the budget of a federal government that had few responsibilities except for defense.

There has been a concerted effort to convince average Americans that they are feeling a financial pinch because their tax dollars are going to people who do not work, who do not deserve financial support, and who will continue to "take" as long as they can. This campaign has been quite successful. Hardworking Americans are indignant that they have been exploited in this way by bleeding heart liberals. This line of reasoning has hit a nerve with the American people. They see evidence all around them that they are being taken advantage of. You can find data on the internet which supposedly proves that this is not the case. We are not paying welfare to people who are in America illegally say these studies. We are not giving refugees cars using the dollars of working Americans. But many American citizens do not believe the data. They believe that the data has been faked. Even though their own sample of "cases" is quite small they trust their senses more than the numbers.

The America people see the Conservatives as tougher when it comes to foreign affairs and they have been convinced that Conservatives are more patriotic than Liberals. Conservatives are given no responsibility for trade deals that we have made which may have helped employers leave America. Having a TV channel that cheerleads for your party and disses the other party has been very beneficial in terms of getting over the giant bump of taking us into the Iraq War in a country that was supposedly awash in weapons, but actually had no such hidden stashes.

It is unclear if people who claim to be Republicans right now all agree with the agenda of the Republican Party or if they just agree about what they don't like about America in the 21ˢᵗ century. For many of us America has changed almost beyond recognition while also providing us in our day-to-day activities much that is still familiar and beloved. America still has room for families to enjoy each other, to gather and relax or celebrate and to allow grandchildren to know their grandparents. We realize that America was never perfect. There was always misery and sadness to worry about and grieve. However many Americans have been convinced that America is on the edge of ruin and that sadness far outweighs happiness in modern America. This negative view has resulted from a complex constellation of factors, but many feel that the GOP is stoking this malaise in order to exploit it.

To contend that the GOP is undermining the Constitution is a harsh criticism to levy and it is a serious charge, perhaps falling under the label of sedition. Once undermined, how do we restore the Constitution to its position as the document that supports our nation, as the very foundation on which our nation is built? If one party decides to "see through" the document that guides us and twist it to its own advantage, if they no longer abide by the bargains made over the past 225 years, then how will we remain a nation that protects freedom through a system of checks and balances if that system can be subverted?

\\\

Sedition – "In law, sedition is overt conduct, such as speech and organization that tends towards insurrection against the established order. Sedition often includes subversion of a constitution and incitement of discontent (or resistance) to lawful authority. Sedition may include any commotion, though not aimed at direct and open violence against the laws."

https://en.wikipedia.org/wiki/Sedition

Chapter 2

Obstruction in the Senate, the Filibuster, and the Courts

The more I learn about our government both past and present the more I understand how contentious things have always been even before the Constitution was ratified. The general idea was that opposing views would get aired through debate and through written essays, articles and what we would today call the public press or the media – that our representatives would reflect the same conflicting views of the day and that these would be hashed out in Congress or in Committees until either a consensus or a compromise was reached. Passions have apparently often run high and tempers have flared. There have been rare moments when events brought our parties together and Congress worked in concert to make laws that would benefit all Americans and perhaps even the entire world. I can think of the Great Depression and World War II.

The Filibuster

The filibuster has been used by both parties to try to table laws that were unpopular with one group or another pretty much permanently. Filibusters are not addressed in our Constitution.

"In 1789, the first U.S. Senate adopted rules allowing the Senate to move the previous question which meant ending debate and proceeding to a vote. Former Vice President Aaron Burr argued in 1806 that the motion regarding the previous question was redundant, had only been exercised once in the preceding four years, and should be eliminated. In that same year, the Senate agreed, recodifying its rules, and thus the potential for a filibuster sprang into being. Because the Senate created no alternative mechanism for terminating debate, the filibuster became an option for delay and blocking of floor votes.

The filibuster remained a solely theoretical option until the late 1830s. The first Senate filibuster occurred in 1837. In 1841, a defining moment came during debate on a bill to charter the Second Bank of the United States. Senator Henry Clay tried to end debate via majority vote. Senator William R. King threatened a filibuster, saying that Clay "may make his arrangements at his boarding house for the winter". Other senators sided with King, and Clay backed down.

(Attributions have been omitted because they are distracting but can be found at Wikipedia,)

"The filibuster or the threat of a filibuster," says Wikipedia, "remains an important tactic that allows a minority to affect legislation. The perceived threat of a filibuster has tremendously increased since the 1960s, as suggested by the increase in cloture motions filed. A motion for cloture is filed not only to overcome filibusters in progress, but also to pre-empt ones that are only anticipated. In the 1960s, no Senate term had more than seven votes on cloture. By the first decade of the 21st century, the number of votes on cloture per Senate term had risen to no fewer than forty-nine. The 110th Congress broke the record for cloture votes, reaching 112 at the end of 2008.

The Senate is the chamber that makes use of the filibuster and they cannot even agree about any part of the process. Wikipedia describes the origins of the "nuclear option", and the ensuing rise of another group who thought this should be called the "constitutional option".

"In 2005, a group of Republican senators led by Senate Majority Leader Bill Frist, responding to the Democrats' threat to filibuster some judicial nominees of President George W. Bush to prevent a vote on the nominations, floated the idea of having Vice President Dick Cheney, as President of the Senate, rule from the chair that a filibuster on judicial nominees was inconsistent with the constitutional grant of power to the president to name judges with the advice and consent of the Senate (interpreting "consent of the Senate" to mean "consent of a simple majority of Senators," not "consent under the Senate rules"). Senator Trent Lott, the junior Republican senator from Mississippi, had named the plan the "nuclear option." Republican leaders preferred to use the term "constitutional option," although opponents, including Senator Barack Obama, the junior senator from Illinois, and some supporters of the plan continued to use "nuclear option." In 2005, Obama opposed the change before supporting it in 2013. He said on the Senate floor "I urge my Republican colleagues not to go through with changing these rules. In the long run it is not a good result for either party. One day Democrats will be in the majority again and this rule change will be no fairer to a Republican minority than it is to a Democratic minority." In 2013, Obama supported the rule change as a Democratic President when Democrats were the majority in the Senate."

https://en.wikipedia.org/wiki/Filibuster_in_the_United_States_Senate

You can get lost in the language of the Senate as with most legalese, and into the weeds on the details. Most people don't bother to tune in because it is a part of the internal procedure in the Senate. The way Senators explain what is happening on the floor of the Senate may even be designed to obfuscate about who is doing what to whom.

The way Senators manipulate procedures can be used as a blame game that relies on the hope that American citizens will get confused by the complexities and have no idea who is blocking a bill and if they are doing it for sound political reasons or for more self-serving reasons. The reasons why Senators filibuster, or invoke cloture, may have a lot to do with Party ideology, or with the majority party feeling empowered with a "mandate" (which used to mean a majority of all the people, and now just refers to the most vocal majority of their own base).

Sometimes Party loyalties are even determined by big donors, or big corporations, or groups of lobbyists. We all can see examples of corruption in our government but we try to remind ourselves that human beings are imperfect and that power will always attract power and money. We the people are meant to be vigilant so that corruption does not get out of hand. Often though we feel powerless to fight wealthy officials and those who befriend them and we forget to raise our voices. There may be those who are elected to govern us who rely on us to get frustrated and to tune out.

So, although the filibuster was not in the original US Constitution it came into existence almost at the birth of our nation. When government was quite small and all of the participants knew each other they perhaps did not always require formal rules to untangle thorny issues so we are told that it was not used as intended until

1841. Today the filibuster has become all too common as a way to stop the business of a minority party when the representation in the Senate is very uneven or when feelings are running really high (as in the day when the Civil Rights Act was being considered). The number of cloture motions (used to stop a filibuster) is often cited as a way to determine how often Senators intended to invoke the filibuster rule. Others say that cloture motions also are used for other things and that such a count is not reliable.

http://www.msnbc.com/morning-joe/obama-gop-has-blocked-500-bills

http://hotair.com/archives/2014/05/09/four-pinocchios-to-obama-for-500-republican-filibusters-claim/

The Filibuster and the Courts

No matter who is counting there has been unprecedented use of the filibuster since Barrack Obama lost the majority for his Party in the Senate and this became such an issue with accusations of obstruction flying through the media and denials also flying and making it clear that we no longer had a single media, but we now had two, both partisan. When it came to filling seats on the Federal District Courts and especially on the DC District Court the issues finally had to be addressed.

"The current fight over the judiciary has very little to do with the pace by which the administration has nominated potential judges. It has everything to do with a Republican Party that has grown increasingly radical. It's a Party that is oblivious to the last two presidential elections, won fairly handily by a Democrat, and beholden to interests that need a federal bench that tilts heavily rightward – to protect corporate interests. So Republican senators, led by Minority Leader Mitch McConnell (R-Ky), have not taken their constitutional duty to provide advice and consent seriously and abused the filibuster to greatly slow the pace of judicial confirmations. This has led to vacancies across the country hovering above 80 for far too long…

The Republican obstructionists' actions have likely had the most adverse effect on the D.C. Circuit, where they recently filibustered one of Obama's selections for the D.C. Circuit, which hears some of the most important constitutional matters of any of the federal appeals circuits. It hears, for instance, challenges to new regulations aimed at enforcing the Clean Air and Clean Water federal laws. It is also a Court that tilts rightward and has shown great hostility to regulations aimed at protecting our environment – good for corporate interests, harmful to the health of many Americans."

Caitlin Halligan, and another of the president's nominees to the D. C. Circuit court, Sri Srinivasan have been waiting so long for consideration that Caitlin is no longer available, although Srinivasan was eventually seated on the court.

http://www.acslaw.org/acsblog/radical-republicans-not-the-president-have-created-the-judicial-vacancy-crisis#.UWHErTkatlg

This graph clearly shows that the filibuster and cloture motions increased precipitately during the Obama years.

http://theweek.com/speedreads/454162/rise-filibuster-maddening-chart

Rise of the Filibuster

Cloture motions filed per legislative session

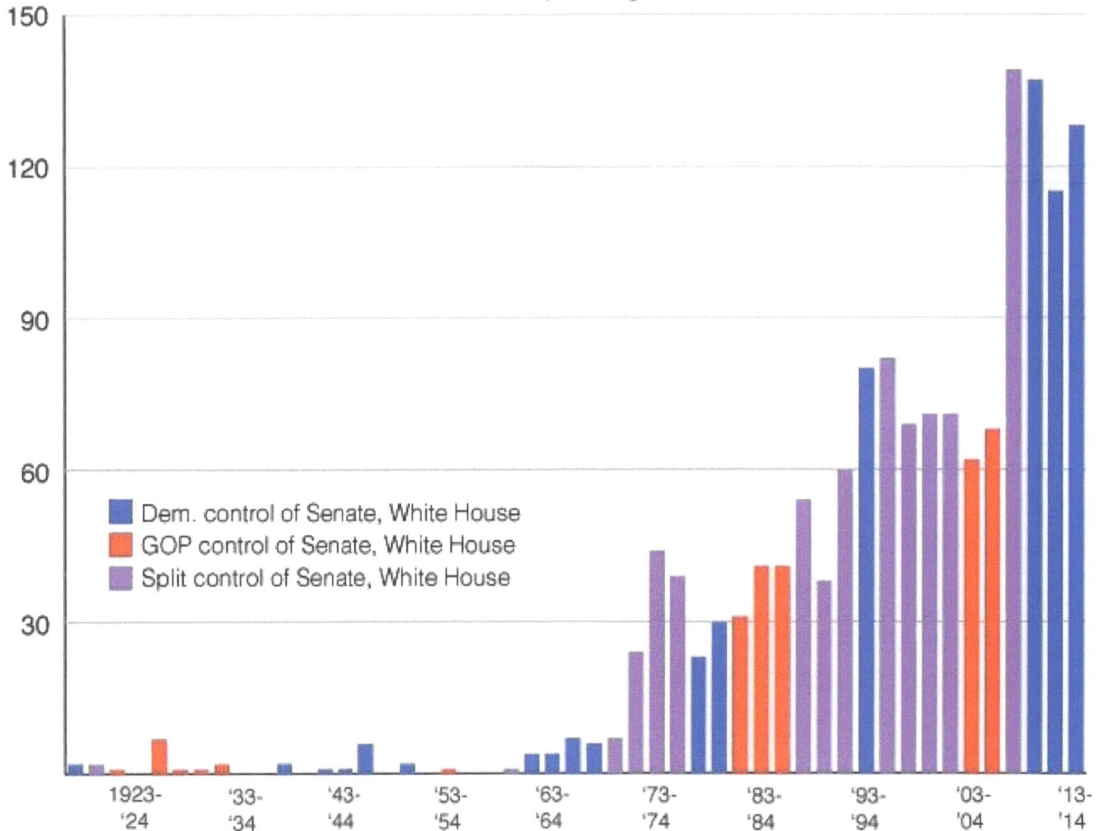

Legend:
- Dem. control of Senate, White House
- GOP control of Senate, White House
- Split control of Senate, White House

X-axis labels: 1923-'24, '33-'34, '43-'44, '53-'54, '63-'64, '73-'74, '83-'84, '93-'94, '03-'04, '13-'14

Y-axis: 30, 60, 90, 120, 150

The filibuster issue as it related to court appointments finally peaked in 2013. It was even suggested that we switch to that "nuclear option" using a simple majority for all decisions about what bills to bring to the floor and to voting Presidential appointments up or down. It was decided that the rule would only change for considering appointments to important government posts and to the courts. For all other bills the original laws would pertain.

Reasons for Obstructing

Were the Republicans obstructing President Obama as racists or were they trying to keep the courts in the hands of Conservatives? We may never know. Perhaps GOP Senators each had his/her own reasons for such blatantly obstructive policies which kept the Senate from doing much business at all, and made every piece of business, like raising the debt ceiling or allowing the deficit to increase, fraught. Clearly they could have had dual or even multiple purposes in their obstructionist strategies.

The threats to shut down the government every time the GOP was forced to tackle business which it found distasteful, we were supposed to believe, were due to fiscal Conservatism. Such disruptive acts upset all Americans and took our own divisiveness up several notches. The Republicans used every tool in the Constitution and a few that would have astounded our forefathers to keep President Obama and the Democrats from changing much of anything from the way George W. Bush and the GOP left it. They wanted to be sure that when they won the next Presidential election they would not have to undo what might be popular Democrat initiatives before they could begin on their own campaign to get out from under the burden of the poor and force them to stand on their own two feet. They also had made complex plans for how they would get back in the White House which was looking harder and harder for Republicans to do since they had pretty effectively angered large segments of voting Americans.

Although the Senate logjam on court appointments was broken up when the nuclear option was put in place, specifically and only for government appointments and although the balance in the courts has swung to the left, these new center left judges do not have the seniority or the heft of the Conservative judges who have been in those courts for so long. Also President Obama tends to favor appointing judges that are closer to the center of the left rather than the liberal fringes while Republicans have tended to appoint judges who hold very Conservative views.

"The reason they want to put more judges on the D.C. Circuit is not because it needs them," Senate Republican leader Mitch McConnell said. He quoted an administration ally who had acknowledged that "the president's best hope for advancing his agenda is through executive action, and that runs through the D.C. Circuit."

Liberal activists have another explanation for GOP obstruction. "It's the farm team," says Nan Aron, president of the liberal Alliance for Justice, of the court's historic role as stepping-stone to the Supreme Court. "Republicans have always fought holy wars over filling those seats."

Despite that setback, Democrats' steady progress on other appeals and district courts has not been denied. It's been a long time coming; Obama, preoccupied by two Supreme Court nominations in his first two years, got a slow start on filling lower court vacancies. Senate Republicans have been even slower to confirm his nominees.

Lining the federal bench with judges who enjoy lifetime tenure is one of the most significant perks of the presidency. Two-term presidents generally appoint nearly 40% of the 874 federal judges. George W. Bush's preference for ideological conservatives remade the judiciary in his image. Obama, with 208 confirmed judges so far, has preferred moderates."

http://www.usatoday.com/story/news/politics/2013/10/31/obama-judges-democrat-republican-senate/3286337/

Republicans used the filibuster, which is a constitutional process, even if no such procedure was described in the original document, to undermine the Constitution by bringing governance to a virtual standstill and an actual series of stand offs. I classify their actions as seditious. Perhaps our dueling forefathers would have been more entertained by modern mock dueling, although they would have feared for how our Constitution might fare in this modern battle over the Constitution. Our Senators have used the Constitution which is supposed to keep our government moving to stop governance and this undermines the power of the document. Senators have duties to the nation and when they subvert the Constitutional tools to avoid doing these duties they disrespect and disembowel the Constitution they are sworn to uphold.

Chapter 3

Obstruction in the House – The Hastert Rule

Obstruction in the US House of Representatives became most obvious after the 113th Congress began. Nothing could get passed. Bills did not even come to the floor. I always had in my mind Mitch McConnell's pledge, made right after the inauguration of President Obama, to stop the President from accomplishing anything while he was in office, but, of course, for the first two years of Obama's first term, 2008-10, Obama had a majority in Congress. Much of that time was eaten up with turning around the economy after the Great Recession and getting the Affordable Care Act passed into law.

In the 2012 election Obama's majorities in Congress became a thing of the past and by the time the 113th Congress took their seats in 2013 obstruction was at peak levels. In the Senate, as we have already discussed Republicans, used a filibuster level set at 60 votes to stop almost all business including the appointments that President Obama had the right and duty to make, appointments to vacancies in the Federal District Courts and to government posts. But nothing was getting through in the House either due to the use of the Hastert rule which said that the Speaker should not bring to the floor of the House any bill that had less than a majority of the majority party willing to vote for it. In the House, after 2010, Republicans were the majority party.

Wikipedia publishes these very useful visuals making who held the majority in each Congress easy to see.

United States Senate

United States
House of Representatives

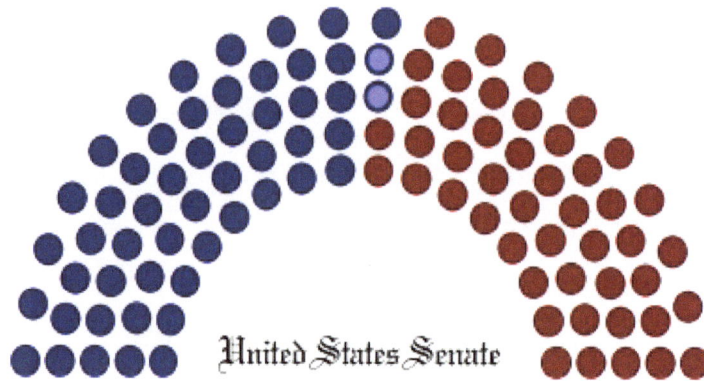

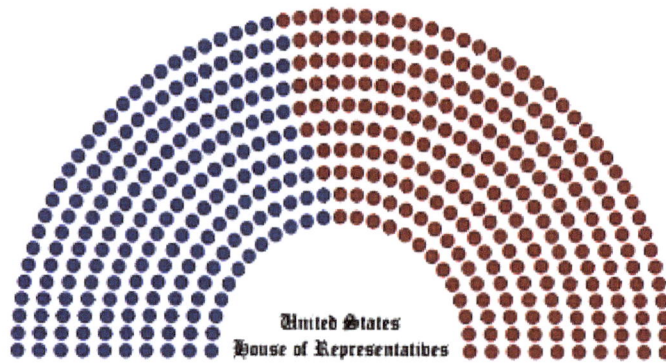

https://en.wikipedia.org/wiki/112th_United_States_Congress

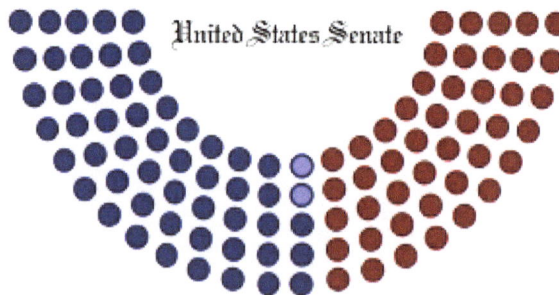

United States Senate

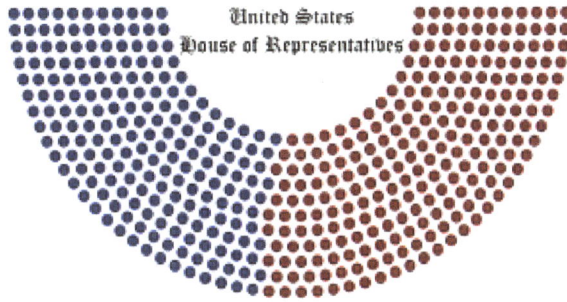

United States
House of Representatives

https://en.wikipedia.org/wiki/113th_United_States_Congress

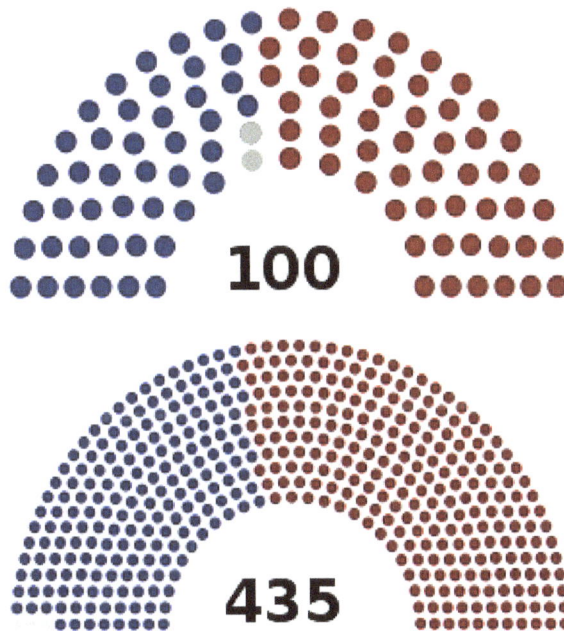

100

435

https://en.wikipedia.org/wiki/114th_United_States_Congress

The Pew Research Center collected and charted this data showing Congressional Productivity in December of 2013.

Congressional Productivity

Laws enacted by each Congress in first year of its two-year term, by type

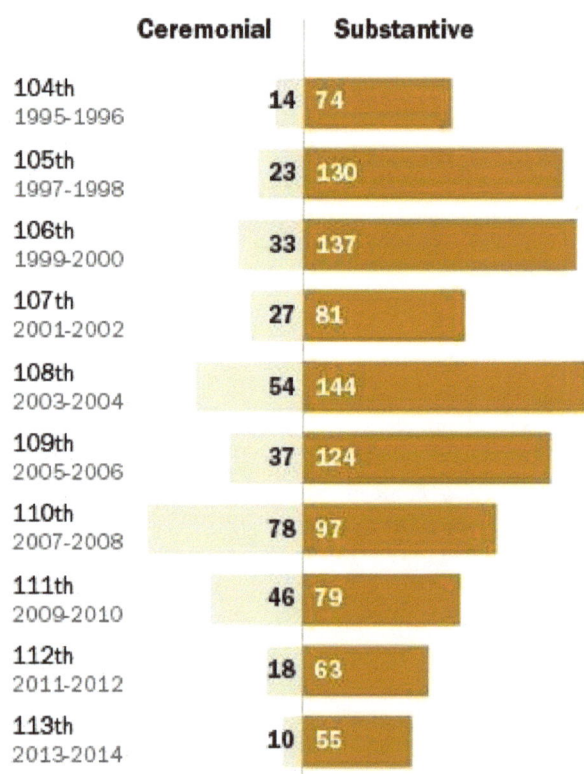

	Ceremonial	Substantive
104th 1995-1996	14	74
105th 1997-1998	23	130
106th 1999-2000	33	137
107th 2001-2002	27	81
108th 2003-2004	54	144
109th 2005-2006	37	124
110th 2007-2008	78	97
111th 2009-2010	46	79
112th 2011-2012	18	63
113th 2013-2014	10	55

Note: Figures for the current (113th) Congress are as of Dec. 23.
Source: Library of Congress' THOMAS website

PEW RESEARCH CENTER

http://www.pewresearch.org/fact-tank/2013/12/23/congress-ends-least-productive-year-in-recent-history/

On 12/23/13 in The Armchair Observer I wrote this about the Hastert Rule:

Dennis Hastert says that there is no Hastert Rule and I think I finally get what he is saying. When you are the Speaker of the House it has been common to pre-count the number of votes in favor of a particular bill. We know Nancy Pelosi often talked about how many votes favored a piece of House business and in fact she was famous both for getting votes from both sides of the aisle and for accurately totaling votes before a bill was brought up on the floor for an up or down vote. But Dennis Hastert, when he was speaker, liked to know how many in his own party (he is a Republican) were in favor of a bill before it was brought to the floor of the House and he liked to know that enough Republicans favored a bill that they could pass it without help from across the aisle. This did not mean that he did not accept bipartisan support for bills; he just liked the idea that a majority of the majority favored making the bill a law.

The Hastert Rule is a rule of practice, not a rule of law. It is not written anywhere, nor has it ever been up for a vote. This is why we can't skirt around the Hastert rule the way we can skirt around the option in the Senate [filibuster rules]. The filibuster rule was a written rule and it could be overturned. You cannot overturn a rule that is just an informal way to conduct business. John Boehner and the current crop of Republicans in the House have seen fit to use the Hastert rule to obstruct the business of the House. Speaker Boehner will only bring a bill to the floor of the House for an up or down vote if it will pass with only Republican votes; if it is acceptable to a majority of the majority. Since Republican policy makers have dictated that no bills favored by any Democrats can reach the floor of the House, Boehner has used the Hastert rule to make it so.

…

They have done all of this because the Democrats made them so angry that they just couldn't help themselves. They have also done this because it suited their agenda. They have raged and insulted and they have damaged the institutions they took oaths to serve. The Republicans in Congress have acted like a pair of tractor trailer truck drivers, arrogant and selfish, who block both lanes of a two-lane highway on purpose and, while they ignore the traffic and the angry drivers stacked up behind them, enjoy acting like they haven't a care in the world as they sign and smile to each other and consolidate their power and control. And they look forward to seeing how long they can keep this up (until the ambulance or the police arrive, and perhaps beyond).

So we cannot undo the Hastert rule. There is no "nuclear" option here. Only John Boehner can stop using the Hastert rule in the way that he has been using it and give up the vendetta, stand down the threat level, and take the American House of Representatives back to business as usual, back to letting bills come to the floor of the House for an up or down vote. The way our Congress works the blockade could still continue even with only one tractor trailer if you imagine that the truck is on a narrow mountain road with double solid lines and it is weaving back and forth.

…

http://thearmchairobserver.com/one-tool-of-obstruction-down-one-to-go/

If the Speaker of the House happens to be a Republican these days and if that Speaker defies the Hastert Rule (which supposedly is a nonbinding strategy) s/he will not remain Speaker for long.

""If you pass major bills without the majority of the majority," Hastert aide John Feehery explained to The Washington Post, "then you tend not to be a long-term speaker."

…

The Senate, with its filibusters, six-year terms, and arcane customs, was envisioned as a deliberative body that would rein in the passions of the day. The House of Representatives—the "people's House"—was supposed to be a more streamlined and responsive legislative body. James Madison, one of the key framers of the Constitution, described the House as having "an immediate dependence on, and intimate sympathy with, the people."

Nobody is seriously saying the Hastert Rule is unconstitutional. But it is ahistorical and, at this point in U.S. political history, often unrepresentative.

Instead of being the "people's House," it's a special-interest-group-controlled fiefdom run autocratically by whichever of the two polarized parties happens to hold the reins. And in the case of immigration reform, it's natural for Obama to feel that Congress is thwarting elective democracy instead of promoting it."

http://www.realclearpolitics.com/articles/2014/11/30/down_with_the_hastert_rule_12478 2.html#ixzz4KpKsnjTm

Wikipedia as a source is often suspect, but in certain public matters of record it is very useful. In this case Wikipedia lists for us the times when John Boehner went against his own party and the Hastert Rule, that they insisted he should heed in order to pass important legislation or to avoid radical moves that the 113th Congress favored like shutting down the government to avoid raising the debt ceiling, etc. Boehner knew he would probably lose his job which he got through a majority vote of his peers, but he defied party leaders and disrupters to pass these measures:

- In December 2012 Boehner told his caucus in a conference call "I'm not interested in passing something with mostly Democrat votes" and that did not have the support of the majority of the Republican caucus. Nonetheless, Boehner allowed a vote on January 1, 2013 on the American Taxpayer Relief Act of 2012 (also known as the "fiscal cliff bill") with only 85 out of 241 Republicans in favor (a support level of only 35%) and the bill passed with the support of 90% of Democrats (172 out of 191). The bill's passage marked the first time in more than ten years that a measure passed a Republican-controlled House when opposed by a majority of House Republicans. In response, former House Speaker Hastert criticized Boehner for not adhering to the "majority of the majority" governing principle by saying, "Maybe you can do it once, maybe you can do it twice, but when you start making deals when you have to get Democrats to pass the legislation, you are not in power anymore."

- Two weeks later, on January 15, 2013, Boehner allowed a vote on aid to victims of Hurricane Sandy to take place without the support of a majority of the Republican caucus. The vote passed with 241 votes, but only 49 of the votes were from Republicans or a mere 21% of the majority.

Since then some notable Republicans have publicly questioned whether the "majority of the majority" rule is still viable or have proposed jettisoning it altogether.

- In spite of all the criticism, on February 28, 2013 Boehner brought a third bill for a vote on the floor of the house which did not have support of majority of Republicans. The bill, an extension of the <u>Violence Against Women Act</u>, received the vote of only 38% of the Republicans in the House of Representatives.

- On April 9, 2013, the "rule" was violated a fourth time, on a bill about federal acquisition of historic sites. The bill was passed with more than two thirds of the House vote but without a majority of the GOP caucus. Shortly thereafter, Boehner said, "Listen: It was never a rule to begin with. And certainly my prerogative – my intention is to always pass bills with strong Republican support."

- On October 16, 2013, Boehner again violated the rule by allowing a floor vote to reopen the government and raise the <u>debt ceiling</u>. The House voted 285 to 144 less than three hours after the Senate overwhelmingly passed the <u>Continuing Appropriations Act, 2014</u>. The "yea" votes consisted of 198 Democrats and only 87 Republicans, less than 40% of the conference.

- On February 11, 2014, Boehner broke the rule by allowing a floor vote on a "clean" <u>debt ceiling</u> bill. The bill passed the house 221-201, with only 28 Republicans voting "yea" along with 193 Democrats.

<u>https://en.wikipedia.org/wiki/Hastert_Rule</u>

Both parties have their ways to block legislation if they are against it and think it might pass if brought up for a vote. This is hardly a departure from either law or tradition. Our forefathers had strategies for doing the same. But to declare up front, as soon as a President from the opposing party is elected that your party will do all in their power to stop the President elected by the people from governing is a departure from previous law and practice. If this happened in every administration our government would collapse. Since no bills could be passed or any business conducted government would essentially be dead.

Grover Norquist, a Libertarian and head of the Americans for Tax Reform group, said that he wants a government that is so small "you can drown it in a bathtub." Since Republicans all signed this pledge is that their motivation for obstruction? They insist that we should make our government smaller because our Federal government is usurping the powers of the States, but do they really expect to go back to 1783 and take an entirely different path? Do you get to take "The Road Not Taken" without unleashing unintended consequences? The Republicans are fairly serious about this as we will discuss later when we look at what they have been up to in the individual states.

Since President Obama is our first American President of African Descent could their motives be classified as racist? We can assume, since they seem to wish to put a Republican back in the White House, that they actually were not trying to get rid of the Federal government completely. Republicans seem convinced that their agenda in areas like the economy and immigration, health care, etc. absolutely will be better for America than the policies espoused by Democrats. Since none of these are areas where there is any absolute proof that the Republican approach will be superior, and in fact there are some facts floating around the internet which suggest that Democrats do better in these areas, that leaves us with the possibilities that Republicans either are blinded by their own ideology or that they are, indeed, racist. Or I suppose it could be that they just like to win and their strategies have nothing to do with what is best for America.

Clearly the data available shows that fewer bills have been passed by the House of Representatives when the Republicans have been the majority party during the Obama years.

http://washingtonmonthly.com/2013/04/05/the-do-little-house-of-representatives-why-so-little-legislating/

House legislative activity (1990-2013)
(early in session)

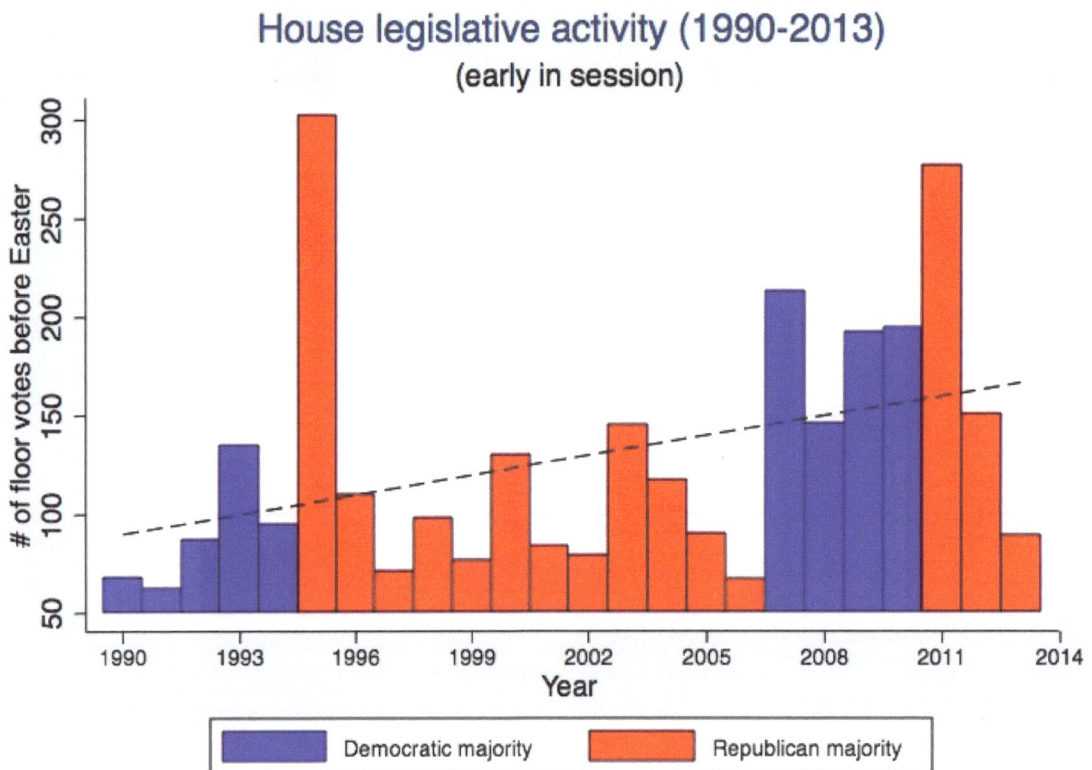

Bills Enacted
First Session of Each Congress Since 1973

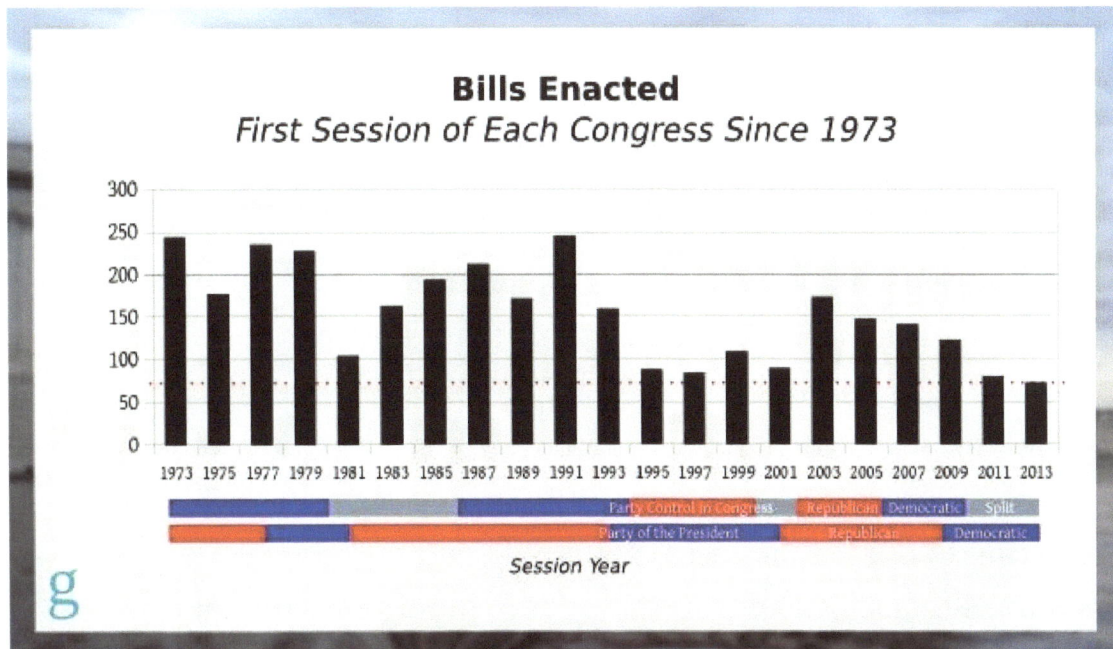

https://www.govtrack.us/blog/category/analysis/

Facts are Mutable

Some people will believe the things I have said about obstruction in the Obama years, some will not. That is how we behave in America now. Facts are mutable. We are somehow in a counterfactual age even with the ability to fact check everything on the internet. In fact the internet is part of the problem. Everyone seems to have their own facts. You can find media that is right leaning, left leaning and very little in the middle. If you are a Conservative you read the articles that you agree with. Democrats do the same thing. Each group even has their own graphics to refer to. Somewhere there is still truth, but just try to prove it. Some people know that facts can be cherry-picked and that if they are you can prove anything. Some people just like to stay in their bubble and believe.

The mutability of facts does not bode well for our Constitution which is treated in the same manner as "facts" on the internet. You can interpret the points our forefathers made in different ways depending on your point of view. The ancestors left room for interpretation on purpose because they wanted the Constitution to be a living document and a lasting document.

The right thinks the section of our Constitution that tells the respective duties of the Federal government and the states is being misinterpreted and has been revised too often by law and tradition so they advocate a return to only the duties literally outlined for the Federal government in the Constitution. All other duties, they say, according to our forefathers belong to the states. They believe that we need to keep hacking off pieces of the Federal government until it is "pure" once again. Republicans are big on what they call purity.

Democrats feel that we should use the Constitution as it has evolved, use it as the living and changing document it is, a document that reflects the changes in American society over the decades. They are not advocating a smaller Federal government, although we all always talk about getting rid of waste in government.

Who is right? Well if we knew what facts were any more then that might help us decide, except that the Conservatives are suggesting that we take the path we did not take and there is no data on that (even if data became nonpartisan again). Which path will keep our Constitution strong and which will hollow it out? Without backtracking and changing everything up and waiting a century how can we know? Chaos will ensue at the very least.

Chapter 4

Amendment 1 – Freedom of Religion, Press, Expression. Ratified 12/15/1791

Congress shall make no law respecting an establishment of religion, or prohibiting the free exercise thereof; or abridging the freedom of speech, or of the press; or the right of people peaceably to assemble, and to petition the Government for a redress of grievances.

Winning in the States

A Bloodless Coup

With a Democrat sitting close by in the White House and a Supreme Court that leaned way to the right, but still not far enough for Republicans, the GOP made one assault after another on the US Constitution during the Obama years in order to turn even our founding documents into instruments of the far right wing. They may have angrily expressed a desire to get even with Obama for being both too strong and too weak, for getting the ACA through Congress, for signing too many executive actions (a charge that is not backed up by real data), but their actions are too coordinated, their attacks come on too many fronts to be merely reactive. These actions are the results of careful planning by Conservative think tanks and Conservative action groups.

Constitutional Laws have been under constant attack and due to the composition of the Supreme Court many battles have been won, although there have been a few loses bemoaned with exaggerated outrage. The basic wording of the original Constitution has not been changed. Most of the attempts have been made against sections like the Federal vs. State's rights sections which our forefathers left somewhat undefined to begin with. The Amendments to our Constitution and the body of law that now trails along with it after 200 years of governance have been the main focus of Conservatives. We are seeing the First Amendment interpretations in flux, the Second Amendment has certainly been in their crosshairs, the Voting Rights Act has received their "loving" attentions, Roe v Wade is under constant siege, even the separation of church and state, long accepted as a given is today a matter for debate.

When we have free speech it seems that nothing is ever truly decided for all time. We continue to think about our laws and to have opinions about them and we do have the freedom to change them. But there are rules. If changing a rule is something that our Congress cannot agree on then the old rule must be followed until a change is actually made.

Extreme Gerrymandering

But suppose that one party has come up with a plan to get around our laws and our processes. Suppose Republicans have used their right to gerrymander districts based on new census numbers (a right that is given to the party in power whenever census data is released) to create districts that are very homogeneous. Extremely gerrymandered districts are obvious on maps because of their very irregular boundaries. Once the gerrymandered districts were drawn by separating voters along party lines the GOP then set about making it more difficult for people who did not usually vote Republican to get to the polls and vote. In a few cases courts have forced the party to redraw districts with the most extreme gerrymandering. It's all factual, well-documented on and off the internet. What they did is technically legal, but attempting to stack votes in your favor is hardly in the spirit of our Constitution.

"Stacking" the Supreme Court

What if one party has a plan to keep the Supreme Court stacked towards one political view, to make the Supreme Court a partisan body? This is also what the Conservatives did. This is one of the reasons they were so angry when we elected such a popular Democrat because this would change the configuration of the Supremes and the Conservatives would lose their edge in the court.

They had big plans for the highest court in the land. Elect a Republican President and if you already have a majority in the legislature and the courts you can pass any laws you like, overturn any amendments you please. The Republicans still want this with all their hearts, even enough to accept Donald Trump as the President of America.

Citizens United v the FEC

This next part starts with a story that almost sounds like fiction but which, in the end, is having serious long term effects on our politics. The GOP, well, to be exact, Citizens United made a movie. Their movie was called *Hillary: The Movie* and it told us why Hillary would make a bad President. The Federal Election Commission in the United States District Court for the District of Columbia cited the Bipartisan Campaign Reform Act to rule against the use of the film. These events began in 2008. An injunction against the actions of the FEC was filed by guess who? Citizens United.

"In an attempt to regulate "big money" campaign contributions, the BCRA applies a variety of restrictions to "electioneering communications." Section 203 of the BCRA prevents corporations or labor unions from funding such communication from their general treasuries. Sections 201 and 311 require the disclosure of donors to such communication and a disclaimer when the communication is not authorized by the candidate it intends to support."

From such a seemingly frivolous beginning came those very serious consequences for political campaigns and for the people's ability to wield power somewhat equal to those with greater wealth. The dam broke open to allow corporations to speak as individuals (but with a much bigger budget) in our elections. When the lower court denied the injunction and said the use of the movie was unconstitutional the backers took the issue all the way to the Supreme Court and we had that infamous ruling Citizens United v the FEC

"The majority maintained that political speech is indispensable to a democracy, which is no less true because the speech comes from a corporation."

…

"Justice Scalia also wrote a separate concurring opinion, joined by Justices Alito and Thomas in part, criticizing Justice Stevens' understanding of the Framer's view towards corporations. Justice Stevens argued that corporations are not members of society and that there are compelling governmental interests to curb corporations' ability to spend money during local and national elections."

"Citizens United v. Federal Election Commission." *Oyez*. Chicago-Kent College of Law at Illinois Tech, n.d. Sep 22, 2016. <https://www.oyez.org/cases/2008/08-205>

Here is Wikipedia saying the same things in language that is perhaps a bit easier to understand:

"The United States Supreme Court held (5–4) that freedom of speech prohibited the government from restricting independent political expenditures by a nonprofit corporation. The principles articulated by the Supreme Court in the case have also been extended to for-profit corporations, labor unions and other associations.

In the case, the conservative non-profit organization Citizens United wanted to air a film critical of Hillary Clinton and to advertise the film during television broadcasts, which was a violation of the 2002 Bipartisan Campaign Reform Act, commonly known as the McCain–Feingold Act or "BCRA" Section 203 of BCRA defined an "electioneering communication" as a broadcast, cable, or satellite communication that mentioned a candidate within 60 days of a general election or 30 days of a primary, and prohibited such expenditures by corporations and unions. The United States District Court for the District of Columbia held that §203 of BCRA applied and prohibited Citizens United from advertising the film *Hillary: The Movie* in broadcasts or paying to have it shown on television within 30 days of the 2008 Democratic primaries. The Supreme Court reversed this decision, striking down those provisions of BCRA that prohibited corporations (including nonprofit corporations) and unions from making independent expenditures and "electioneering communications"

...

The Court, however, upheld requirements for public disclosure by sponsors of advertisements (BCRA §201 and §311). The case did not involve the federal ban on direct contributions from corporations or unions to candidate campaigns or political parties, which remain illegal in races for federal office.

So as of 2010 it was fine for corporations to pay for advertising on the media right up to the day of an election, although public disclosure of the source of the ad was also required.

Why do Democrats dislike the Citizens United agreement? Isn't the party also backed by corporations with deep pockets? Is this law which makes something which was unconstitutional into something that is constitutional likely to undermine the document at the foundation of our government? Democrats have that view. They feel that money talks a bit too much in our government and our elections already. The wealthy and powerful hardly needed more wealth and power. Is this a free speech issue? Should corporations speak as people? How many people? Will they eventually be allowed to vote? How many votes? Corporations may be made up of people but whether are not they deserve a right of free speech is a complex issue. The fact that this decision was brought to us courtesy of an injunction against a movie and a stacked Supreme Court has a lot to do with the outcry against it. People want their votes to actually count in elections and we only get one vote each. After this decision our vote seems somehow smaller. I say this is one bad tweak of our Constitution.

Donor Connections to Conservative Organizations

In or around 2013 I happened to find some interesting charts from a site called Muckety.com or MucketyMaps.com that showed the connections among the various Conservative Foundations. This site still functions and they have traced all kinds of connections both Conservative and Liberal. But clearly the right has been almost obsessively organized and all these groups have missions to complete. Most groups have a mission statement and they have certain goals. In this case all of the goals center around things people on the right want, ideas they espouse, strategies they discuss and share. That's a lot of organizing and we are beginning to see some of the ways that this organizing has paid off. We have the Supreme Court leaning right and both Houses of Congress with right wing majorities and we have a big win in Citizens United v the FEC.

Here are a couple diagrams or maps produced by Muckety showing the complexity of connections among right leaning groups:

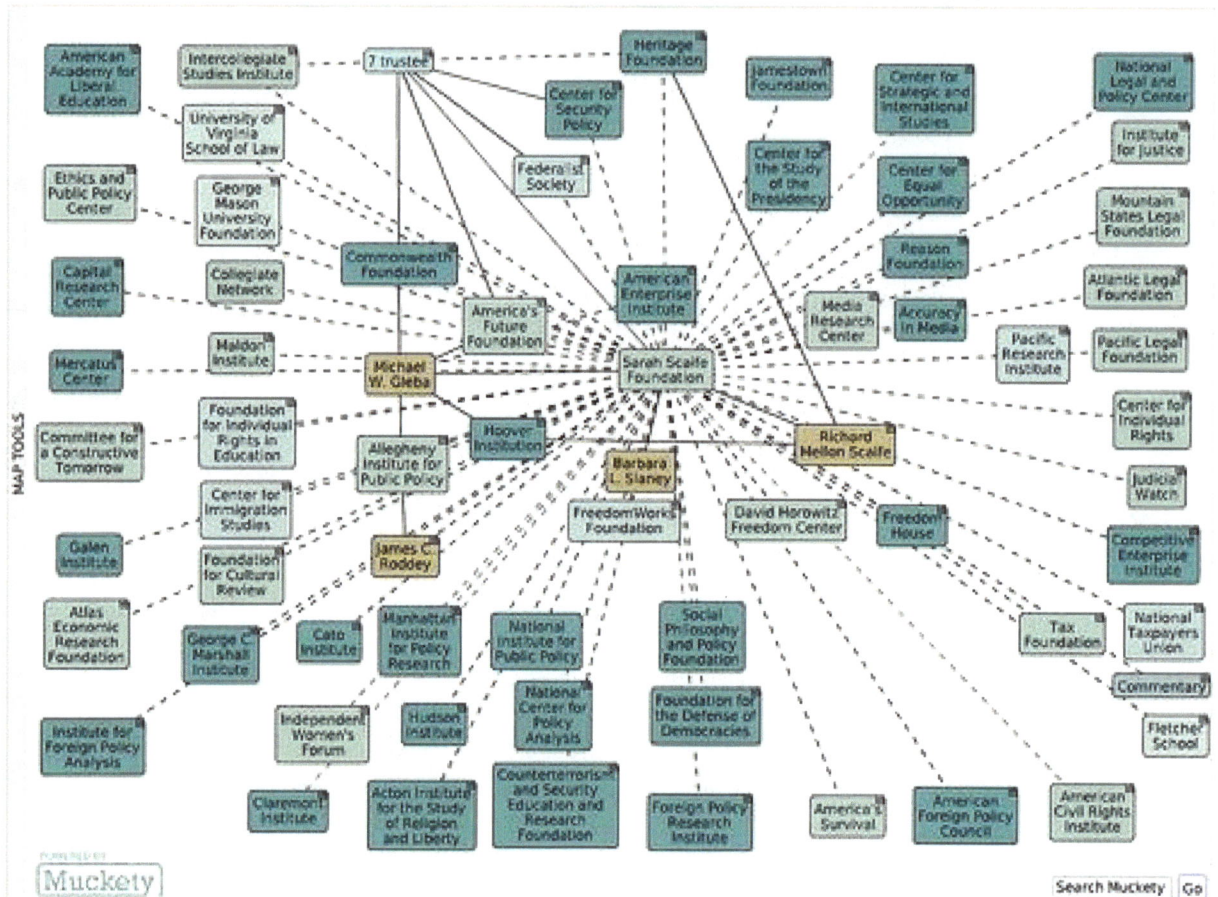

Conservative Foundations

This Conservative Foundations relationship map is interactive. Click around to explore relations in the map.

American Academy for Liberal Education · Intercollegiate Studies Institute · 7 trustee · Heritage Foundation · Jamestown Foundation · Center for Strategic and International Studies · National Legal and Policy Center

University of Virginia School of Law · Center for Security Policy · Center for the Study of the Presidency · Institute for Justice

Ethics and Public Policy Center · George Mason University Foundation · Federalist Society · Center for Equal Opportunity · Mountain States Legal Foundation

Capital Research Center · Collegiate Network · Commonwealth Foundation · American Enterprise Institute · Reason Foundation · Atlantic Legal Foundation

Mercatus Center · Haldon Institute · America's Future Foundation · Michael W. Gleba · Sarah Scaife Foundation · Media Research Center · Accuracy in Media · Pacific Research Institute · Pacific Legal Foundation

Committee for a Constructive Tomorrow · Foundation for Individual Rights in Education · Allegheny Institute for Public Policy · Hoover Institution · Richard Mellon Scaife · Center for Individual Rights

Center for Immigration Studies · Barbara L. Slaney · Judicial Watch

Galen Institute · Foundation for Cultural Review · James C. Roddey · FreedomWorks Foundation · David Horowitz Freedom Center · Freedom House · Competitive Enterprise Institute

Atlas Economic Research Foundation · George C Marshall Institute · Cato Institute · Manhattan Institute for Policy Research · National Institute for Public Policy · Social Philosophy and Policy Foundation · Tax Foundation · National Taxpayers Union

Independent Women's Forum · Hudson Institute · National Center for Policy Analysis · Foundation for the Defense of Democracies · Commentary

Institute for Foreign Policy Analysis · Fletcher School

Claremont Institute · Acton Institute for the Study of Religion and Liberty · Counterterrorism and Security Education and Research Foundation · Foreign Policy Research Institute · America's Survival · American Foreign Policy Council · American Civil Rights Institute

MAP TOOLS

Muckety

Search Muckety [Go]

The following map has the Koch brothers top left and traces their right wing connections:

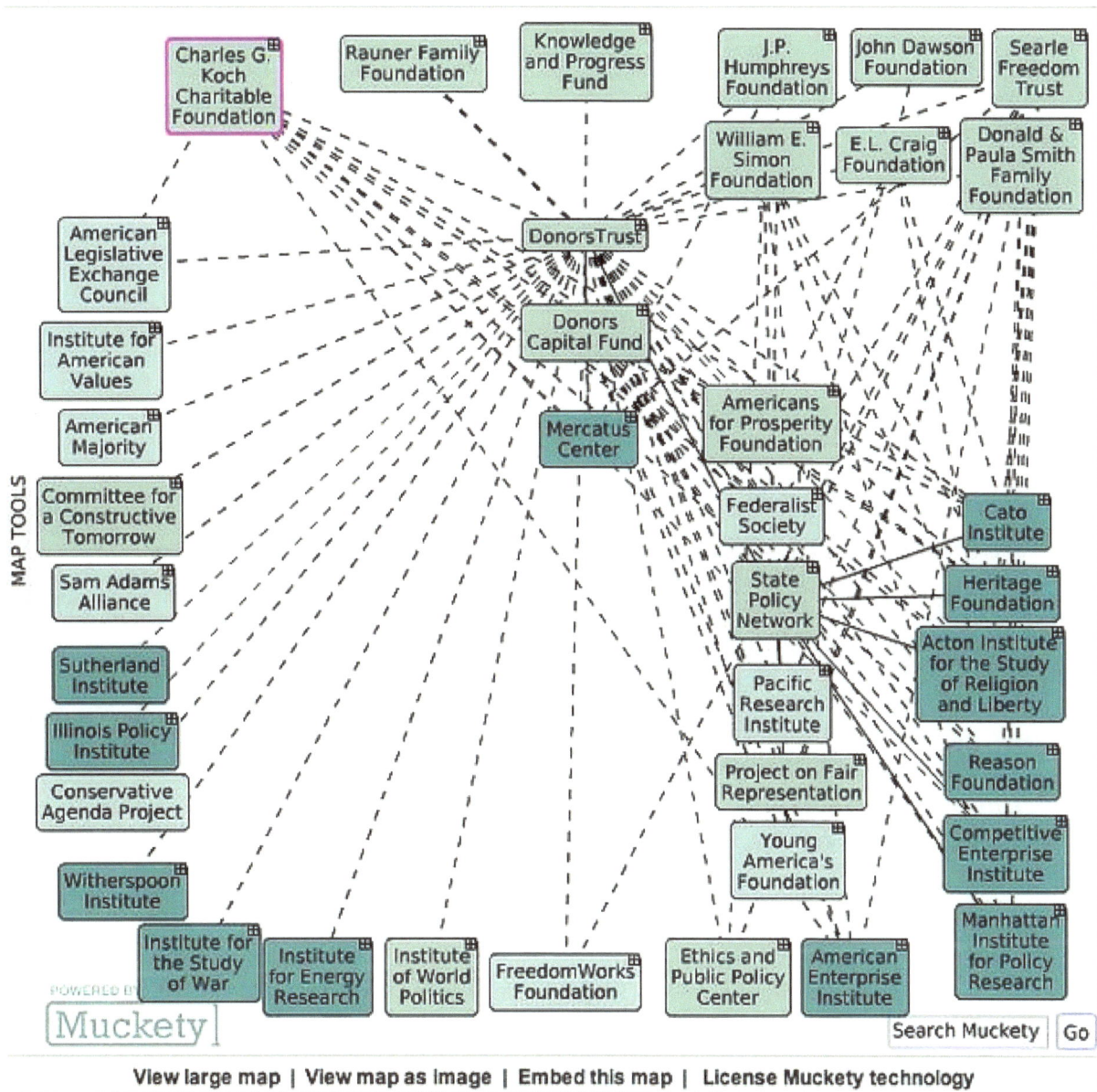

DonorsTrust

You can still find these charts at Muckety.com and some are interactive allowing you to click and point to get more detail.

I include these just in case you don't believe that the Republicans have a "play book", just in case you think all of these small partisan battles won are lucky breaks or some kind of favor granted by the universe. These folks have been at war; there is a plan and the end game is winner take all – the Executive Branch, the Legislative Branch, and the Judicial Branch. This is a fantasy any political party could get behind. It would give a party carte blanche to set the entire agenda for the United States of America for a good long time to come. What else is on the Republican wish list? Well the list is long and inroads have been made but not without rewriting our Constitutional body of documents, laws and traditions.

McCutcheon v the FEC

Before the shock of the Court's decision on Citizens United and the granting of peoplehood to corporations had even settled the Conservatives had to get rid of those pesky limits on contributions. So we had the aftershock of McCutcheon v the FEC decisions delivered another blow to citizens who are not wealthy.

"McCutcheon v. Federal Election Commission, 572 U.S. ___ (2014), is a landmark campaign finance decision of the United States Supreme Court. The decision held that Section 441 of the Federal Election Campaign Act (FECA), which imposed a limit on contributions an individual can make over a two-year period to national party and federal candidate committees, is unconstitutional.

The case was argued before the Supreme Court on October 8, 2013, being brought on appeal after the United States District Court for the District of Columbia dismissed the challenge. It was decided on April 2, 2014, by a 5–4 vote, reversing the decision below and remanding. Justices Roberts, Scalia, Kennedy, and Alito invalidated "aggregate contribution limits" (amounts one can contribute over the two-year period) as violating the First Amendment. Justice Thomas provided the necessary fifth vote, but concurred separately in the judgment while arguing that all contribution limits are unconstitutional."

https://en.wikipedia.org/wiki/McCutcheon_v._FEC

Our forefathers were wealthy compared to other colonists. They owned land and some, sadly, even owned slaves. They were somewhat elitist and they did not really all think that equality meant everyone was equal. "Some", of course, as George Orwell said in **Animal Farm,** "were more equal than others". Even so they did not grant American businesses the right to vote or think of singling them out as having their own freedom of speech. I'm surprised that they did not foresee that people with lots of money would try to influence elections. Perhaps they were too busy inventing our new government, so different from contemporary governments in England and Europe. But in the decades since our founding Congress has made laws about money in politics and the laws they made tended to limit the influence of big money on elections.

Who thought of this little two-stage game changer? Was it in the play book of the Conservatives all along? Did the Koch brothers and other big Conservative donors help design the play book? Were they calling the shots? They all look pretty cozy. There is a book called **Dark Money** by Jane Mayer which speaks of these things.

Regardless of whether this was all planned or some kind of cosmic serendipity the Republicans were thrilled with these two rulings which, added to the other strategies they had planned were designed to help them in the 2014 or 2016 election or even further down the line if necessary.

501 (c) 4's and the IRS Scandal

There was one more loose end in locking down these aggressive and undemocratic campaign finance reforms. It involved two groups of taxpayers delineated by the IRS. One group contains organizations categorized a 501 (c) 3, the other 501 (c) 4. Perhaps you remember this "scandal". 501-c3's are nonprofits like charities and religious groups who do not have to pay taxes but who do have to file paperwork to prove that no taxes are due. 501-c4's are social groups, for profits, associations, groups who do things both tax exempt and not tax exempt. Lots of political organizations on both the left and the right are considered 501-c4's. In order to be tax exempt a 501-c4 cannot do politics all the time. They must have a social or educational function also. Politics can only be 49% or less of what they do.

I'll let Wikipedia summarize the IRS scandal that was related to these two tax groups:

"In 2013, the United States Internal Revenue Service (IRS) revealed that it had selected political groups applying for tax-exempt status for intensive scrutiny based on their names or political themes. This led to wide condemnation of the agency and triggered several investigations, including a Federal Bureau of Investigation criminal probe ordered by United States Attorney General Eric Holder.

Initial reports described the selections as nearly exclusively of conservative groups with terms such as "Tea Party" in their names. According to Republican lawmakers, liberal-leaning groups and the Occupy movement had also triggered additional scrutiny, but at a lower rate than conservative groups. The Republican majority on the House Oversight Committee issued a report, which concluded that although some liberal groups were selected for additional review, the scrutiny that these groups received did not amount to targeting when compared to the greater scrutiny received by conservative groups. The report was criticized by the committee's Democratic minority, which said that the report ignored evidence that the IRS used keywords to identify both liberal and conservative groups.

In January 2014, the FBI told Fox News that its investigation had found no evidence so far warranting the filing of federal criminal charges in connection with the scandal, as it had not found any evidence of "enemy hunting", and that the investigation continued. On October 23, 2015, the Justice Department declared that no criminal charges would be filed."

This article from The Washington Post explains the situation very clearly:

"How much money are they spending?

A lot. And much of is being dished out by conservative groups. According to the Center for Responsive Politics, conservative nonprofits spent more than $263 million during the 2012 campaign, while liberal counterparts spent close to $35 million. A separate Center For Responsive Politics/Center for Public Integrity study found that in 2010, the social welfare nonprofits outspent super PACs by a 3-2 margin.

…

Here's the key difference: Super PACs must disclose their donors while 501(c)(4)s do not. If you are a donor looking to influence election but do not want to reveal your identity, the 501(c)(4) is an attractive option through which to send your cash.

Why has the IRS gotten so many 501(c)(4) applications in recent years?

In 2010, the Supreme Court's landmark "Citizens United" decision cleared the way for corporations and labor unions to raise and spend unlimited sums of money, and register for tax-exempt status under section 501(c)(4). So what happened next is not surprising. The IRS was flooded with applications from groups seeking the special 501(c)(4) designation. Applications more than doubled following the High Court's ruling."

https://www.washingtonpost.com/news/the-fix/wp/2013/05/13/what-is-a-501c4-anyway/

This brouhaha with the IRS got the tax guys off the backs of Conservative groups using 501 (c)4 classifications and let them get on unhindered with the big money they wanted to use in politics to "buy" Federal elections, and since they were getting ready to give more power to the states, and since down ballot elections are what gave them the Legislature, they were also now free to spend large in state and local elections when it seemed politically expedient.

Winning in the States

Their recent wins in the area of campaign finance reform has allowed the Republicans to win big in the individual states. When I looked in 2013 Republicans controlled 23 state governments. Now, in 2016, the number of states controlled all or in part by Republicans in 32. These states were not always what we thought of as "red states" either. Republicans have won the state houses in "blue states" also.

Chris Cillizza sums this up for us in an article he wrote for **The Washington Post** on November 4, 2015 entitled *The 2015 Election Tightened the Republican Stranglehold on State Government.*

The 2015 election is over. (You may not have known it was even happening.) And it proved one thing: Republicans have an absolute stranglehold on governorships and state legislatures all across the country.

…

Republicans now hold 32 of the nation's governorships — 64 percent of all the governors mansions in the country.

…

* Democrats' failure to take over the Virginia state Senate means that Republicans still hold total control of 30 of the country's 50 state legislatures (60 percent) and have total or split control of 38 of the 50 (76 percent.)

That dominance — and what it means to the policy and political calculations and prospects for both parties at the national level — is the single most overlooked and underappreciated story line of President Obama's time in office. Since 2009,

Republicans have made massive and unprecedented gains at the state level, gains that played a central role in, among other things, handing control of the U.S. House back to the GOP in the 2010 election.

It's hard to overstate how important those GOP gains — and the consolidation of them we've seen in the last few years — are to the relative fates of the two parties. While the story at the national level suggests a Republican Party that is growing increasingly white, old and out of step with the country on social issues, the narrative at the local level is very different. Republicans are prospering at the state level in ways that suggest that the party's messaging is far from broken.

There are other, more pragmatic effects of the GOP dominance in governor's races and state legislatures, too. Aside from giving the party a major leg up in the decennial redrawing of congressional lines, which has led to a Republican House majority not only today but likely through at least 2020, the GOP's dominance gives the party fertile ground to incubate policy that makes its way to the national level and to cultivate the future stars of the national party from the ground up.

While the demographic and electoral challenges that Republicans must confront at the national level are very real, the idea, pushed in some circles, that those struggles are leading indicators of a dying party is absolutely wrong. In fact, at the state and local level the Republican Party is considerably more robust than its Democratic counterpart.

Focus on the presidential race exclusively if you will. But remember that the long-term health of a party is about much more than simply the man or woman at the top of the ticket.

https://www.washingtonpost.com/news/the-fix/wp/2015/11/04/the-2015-election-tightened-the-republican-stranglehold-on-state-government/

So while the Republicans have not been busy with the people's business, they have been very busy taking care of their own business. And I am guessing that they are well satisfied with the number of check marks placed against the items in their play book that they have managed to accomplish. The Democrats have not reacted strongly enough to head off the Republican offense. Their defense stinks and they haven't had any offense either.

The results of the 2016 election will tell us how well the Republican assault on campaign rules and laws has worked. However, the things the new rules they have made have already skewed our Constitution towards the right in ways that may affect our nation for a while or forever. What we have seen is that even though we could see what the GOP was up to, since they controlled the Congress, the Courts, and so many state governments we were almost powerless to stop them, despite the fact that our President has been a Democrat. This is exactly why I call this a "bloodless coup". Can the Democrats at least hang on to the Executive Branch? It's looking a bit "iffy".

Chapter 5

Roe v Wade

Defying a Supreme Court Decision

After my Glenn Beck epiphany, after the apocryphal stomach ache brought on by his repeated comparisons between Barrack Obama and Hitler. After he intimated that the enormous crowds Obama attracted in America and in Europe brought to his mind the tainted charisma of Adolph on the rise, I, as I said, started to pay a lot more attention to the news. At first I settled on CNN but eventually I found a home with MSNBC, at least with the mix of commentators they had before they made that major readjustment before the 2016 election, the one that put all the safe white male news anchor types back in charge.

I have been as concerned as many Americans have been by the debate in America over whether Roe v Wade should be supported or overturned. Many of those who object to Roe v Wade and women's right to have abortions and plan their families and use contraception, object for religious reasons. This makes it difficult for the anti-abortion people to get traction because, for most of us, religion and government are separate entities in America.

We have seen activism that has tipped over into violence at times. Doctors who agree to perform abortions are hounded, their home addresses are published for purposes of intimidation, and all these heightened emotions led to death for at least one abortion doctor. Perhaps that is the moment that the "pro-life" (anti-abortion) people decided that they needed to regroup and find less objectionable ways to stop women from being able to get abortions in America.

This is a tale we are all familiar with, in fact we have all taken a side on this issue. Evangelicals and Catholics have teamed up on this issues because they agree along religious lines about when life begins, about which commandment is being broken, and about what will happen to their (immortal) souls if they don't do everything to overturn this evil Supreme Court decision foisted on them by soulless Liberals.

What surprised me when I tuned back into watching news and when I had the time to watch news all day every day was the "war on women" which was clearly being waged, but which Republicans denied. I was not prepared for the rhetoric and I was shocked to find so many Republican men who were happy to appear on TV to say misogynistic things about women and sex. Here are some of the things these men who hold positions of respect in America had to say:

1. **Women are just "hosts" for the precious babies that the GOP suddenly stops caring about once they are born, Virginia Senator Steve Martin said in 2014:**

"I don't expect to be in the room or will I do anything to prevent you from obtaining a contraceptive. However, once a child does exist in your womb, I'm not going to assume a right to kill it just because the child's host (some refer to them as mothers) doesn't want it."

2. **Women who have abortions should be hanged, according to conservative columnist Kevin Williamson:**

3. **Rape and incest are "minor problems" when compared to abortion, GOP strategist Matt Mackowiak mansplained:**

"Texas is a pro-life state. We can get into minor issues that are one percent or two percent the problem. But ultimately, Texas is a strong pro-life state. Abbott would love to fight this campaign on that issue alone from here on out but Wendy knows that's not strategically wise."

Wendy knows that's not strategically wise."

4. "No" doesn't always mean "no" if the man decides it doesn't, says aging right-wing slob Rush Limbaugh:

How many guys, in your own experience with women, have learned that no means yes if you know how to spot it? ... Are these [policies] not lawsuits waiting to happen?

5. Emergency rooms erase rape, claimed Texas Rep. Jodie Laudenberg in 2013:

"If a woman is raped... We have hospital emergency rooms. We have funded what's called rape kits that will help the woman, basically clean her out. And then hopefully that will alleviate that."

6. Oral contraceptives cause prostate cancer…in women…who don't have prostates, so said New Hampshire state Rep. Jeanine Notter in 2012:

"As a man, would it interest you to know that Dr. Brownstein just published an article that links the pill to prostate cancer?"

7. Abortion causes breast cancer, and women should pop out babies as early as possible — a lie so precious Republicans in New Hampshire included it in an anti-abortion bill in 2012:

"In fact, for each year that a woman's first full-term pregnancy is delayed, her risk of breast cancer rises 3.5 percent. The theory that there is a direct link between abortion and breast cancer builds upon this undisputed foundation."

8. Women who use contraception are sluts and prostitutes, so sayeth Rush Limbaugh in response to Sandra Fluke's testimony about a lesbian friend who uses birth control for noncontraceptive medical purposes:

"What does it say about the college co-ed Susan Fluke [sic] who goes before a congressional committee and essentially says that she must be paid to have sex. What does that make her? It makes her a slut, right? It makes her a prostitute. She wants to be paid to have sex. She's having so much sex she can't afford the contraception. She wants you and me and the taxpayers to pay her to have sex."

9. "Legitimate rape," courtesy of Todd Akin:

"From what I understand from doctors, that's really rare. If it's a legitimate rape, the female body has ways to try to shut that whole thing down. But let's assume maybe that

didn't work or something. I think there should be some punishment, but the punishment ought to be on the rapist."

10. Long before "legitimate rape," Bush-appointed federal judge James Holmes said in 1980 that <u>wimmin can't get pregnant from rape</u>:

"Concern for rape victims is a red herring because conceptions from rape occur with approximately the same frequency as snowfall in Miami."

11. Seriously, the <u>"juices don't flow"</u> and pregnancy just doesn't happen if a woman is raped, Republican Rep. Henry Aldridge said in 1995:

"The facts show that people who are raped — who are truly raped — the juices don't flow, the body functions don't work and they don't get pregnant. Medical authorities agree that this is a rarity, if ever."

12. <u>Contraception is as cheap as an aspirin between the knees</u>, Rick Santorum donor foster Freiss said in 2012:

"On this contraceptive thing, my Gosh it's such [sic] inexpensive. You know, back in my days, they used Bayer aspirin for contraception. The gals put it between their knees, and it wasn't that costly."

13. <u>God wanted you to be raped</u>, Republican Senate candidate Richard Mourdock told victims who might want an abortion in 2012:

"I struggled with it myself for a long time, but I came to realize life is that gift from God. And I think even when life begins in that horrible situation of rape, that it is something that God intended to happen."

14. In 2013, Congressman Steve Stockman postulated that <u>if babies had guns, they would kill their mothers rather than be aborted</u>…and ultimately die anyway:

15. Tea Party queen, Saturday Night Live has-been Victoria Jackson, <u>blamed the Sandy hook massacre on abortion</u> in 2012:

"My friend Jim Riley posted: 'Wasn't the Connecticut killer just doing what abortionists do every day?' It's a wonder we don't have more 20 year old "dads" doing what women and doctors have been an accomplice to for years in America. When you forget the TEN COMMANDMENTS, people, THIS is what you get. Obama dramatically wiped a tear as he said, 'the majority of those who died today were children — beautiful little kids …

They had their entire lives ahead of them — birthdays, graduations, weddings, kids of their own... YEAH OBAMA. SAME AS THE MILLION BABIES YOU HAD ABORTED THIS YEAR. ARE YOU CRYING FOR THEM?!"

16. [Fetuses masturbate](#), according to Rep. Michael Burges in 2013:

"Watch a sonogram of a 15-week baby, and they have movements that are purposeful. They stroke their face. If they're a male baby, they may have their hand between their legs. If they feel pleasure, why is it so hard to believe that they could feel pain?"

17. Alabama state Rep. Mary Sue McClurkin said in 2013 that [a fetus should be considered an organ in a woman's body](#):

"When a physician removes a child from a woman, that is the largest organ in a body. That's a big thing. That's a big surgery. You don't have any other organs in your body that are bigger than that."

18. According to Tom Cotton, who [violated the Logan Act](#) in his attempt to throttle a nuclear deal with Iran, said [women should not serve in the military because they're weak](#):

"To have women serving in infantry, though, could impair the mission-essential tasks of those units. And that's been proven in study after study, it's nature, upper body strength, and physical movements, and speed, and endurance, and so forth."

19. [A woman wasn't truly raped if she didn't go to the emergency room immediately](#), according to 2016 presidential candidate Ron Paul:

" If it's an honest rape, that individual should go immediately to the emergency room. I would give them a shot of estrogen or give them –"

20. [Some girls –especially underage ones — "rape easy"](#) according to Wisconsin Republican Roger Rivard:

"If you do (have premarital sex), just remember, consensual sex can turn into rape in an awful hurry. Because all of a sudden a young lady gets pregnant and the parents are madder than a wet hen and she's not going to say, 'Oh, yeah, I was part of the program.' All that she has to say or the parents have to say is it was rape because she's underage. And he just said, 'Remember, Roger, if you go down that road, some girls,' he said, 'they rape so easy.'"

21. "Why not just sit back an enjoy" being raped, wondered Texas Republican Clayton Williams:

"Well, bad weather is like rape: if it's inevitable, you might as well relax and enjoy it."

22. If a woman who was raped wants an abortion, her doctor should make sure she was REALLY raped, said Idaho state Senator Chuck Winder in 2012:

"I would hope that when a woman goes into a physician with a rape issue that that physician will indeed ask her about perhaps her marriage, was this pregnancy caused by normal relations in a marriage, or was it truly caused by a rape."

23. Mike Huckabee would force child rape victims to give birth to, and raise, their rapists' babies:

"Let nobody be misled, a 10-year-old girl being raped is horrible, but does it solve a problem by taking the life of an innocent child?"

24. According to Fox News contributor Liz Trotta, female soldiers should just expect men to rape them:

"The sexual abuse report says that there has been, since 2006, a 64% increase in violent sexual assaults. Now, what did they expect? These people are in close contact, the whole airing of this issue has never been done by Congress, it's strictly been a question of pressure from the feminists."

25. According to Republican Paul Ryan, rape is just another method of conception — like in vitro fertilization, which he wants to criminalize:

"Asked in 2012 if a woman should be able to get an abortion if she is raped, Ryan answered, "I'm very proud of my pro-life record, and I've always adopted the idea that, the position that the method of conception doesn't change the definition of life."

26. To 2016 presidential candidate Mike Huckabee, there's an upside to rape:

"And so I know it happens, and yet even from those horrible, horrible tragedies of rape, which are inexcusable and indefensible, life has come and sometimes, you know, those people are able to do extraordinary things. "

27. Seriously, God really wanted you to be raped because it's a "blessing", Missouri Republican Sharon Barnes said in 2012:

"Abortion is never an option. At that point, if God has chosen to bless this person with a life, you don't kill it."

28. God even planned your rape, explained failed GOP candidate for Senate Sharron Angle in 2010:

"There is a plan and a purpose, a value to every life no matter what it's location, age, gender or disability. So whenever we talk about government and government's role, government's role is to protect life and that's what our Founding Father said, that we have the right to life, liberty and the pursuit of happiness."

29. In fact, Kansas state Rep. Pete DeGraaf said in 2011 that women should probably just go ahead and plan to be raped:

"We do need to plan ahead, don't we, in life?" DeGraaf asked as he supported a piece of anti-choice legislation that would ban insurance companies from including abortion in their general health plans, except when the mother's life is threatened (no rape or incest exceptions) in 2011. "I have spare tire on my car," he mansplained. "I also have life insurance. I have a lot of things that I plan ahead for."

30. Men, after all, have the right to rape women as long as those dirty harlots are allowed to have abortions, according Maine state Rep. Lawrence Lockman in 1995:

"If a woman has [the right to an abortion], why shouldn't a man be free to use his superior strength to force himself on a woman? At least the rapist's pursuit of sexual freedom doesn't [in most cases] result in anyone's death."

31. Besides, if a man rapes a woman and a baby is produced, the woman should feel blessed because of the "gift" God and her rapist gave her, according to 2016 presidential candidate Rick Santorum:

"I think the right approach is to accept this horribly created — in the sense of rape — but nevertheless a gift in a very broken way, the gift of human life, and accept what God has given to you... rape victims should make the best of a bad situation."

32. When it comes down to abortion, a woman does not have the right to her own life, former Republican Rep. Joe Walsh said in 2012:

"Understand though, that when we talk about exceptions, we talk about rape, incest, health of a woman, life of a woman. Life of the woman is not an exception."

33. Former Tea Party candidate for Senate and OB-GYN Greg Brannon mansplained that pregnant women are just "little girls" who don't understand their own bodies like he does:

Brannon described rape crisis centers' clients as *"little girls [who] don't understand what's going on to their bodies."*

34. Did you know that rape exceptions are "little gotcha amendments?" Kansas state Senate Majority Leader Terry Bruce does!:

"These amendments are little gotcha amendments. I'm getting a little irritated at it."

35. Women who are raped should consider that, while rape is bad, the child might be absolutely beautiful, West Virginia Delegate Brian Kurcaba said in 2015:

"Obviously rape is awful," but *"What is beautiful is the child that could come from this."*

36. Rape isn't just for unmarried harlots, though. It's also for husbands, who Utah state Rep. Brian Greene says should be able to rape their wives while they are unconscious. It's not their first date, after all:

"If an individual has sex with their wife while she is unconscious…a prosecutor could then charge that spouse with rape, theoretically. That makes sense in a first-date scenario, but to me, not where people have a history of years of sexual activity."

37. In 2005, conservative commentator William J. Bennett explained that women could decrease the crime rate through abortion — if they aborted black babies:

"If you wanted to reduce crime, you could — if that were your sole purpose — you could abort every black baby in this country, and your crime rate would go down."

38. Women shouldn't vote, according to conservative Ann Coulter:

"If we took away women's right to vote, we'd never have to worry about another Democrat president. It's kind of a pipe dream, it's a personal fantasy of mine, but I don't think it's going to happen. And it is a good way of making the point that women are voting so stupidly, at least single women."

39. You can't be raped if you're married, according to 2016 GOP candidate Donald Trump:

"You cannot rape your spouse. And there's very clear case law."

40. According to right-wing Evangelical "Christian" Pat Robertson, the fight for women's rights has nothing to do with women — it's a socialist plot to destroy the family and kill children, among other things:

"The feminist agenda is not about equal rights for women. It is about a socialist, anti-family political movement that encourages women to leave their husbands, kill their children, practice witchcraft, destroy capitalism and become lesbians."

41. Life might actually begin before conception, so sayeth former Arizona Governor Jan Brewer when she signed a bill that said as much:

The bill defined gestational age as *"calculated from the first day of the last menstrual period of the pregnant woman"* — two weeks prior to conception.

42. But it's OK — 2016 Republican candidate Ben Carson says we should "re-educate" women so they don't get too uppity about abortion:

"What we need to do is re-educate the women to understand that they are the defenders

43. With all this talk about "re-education," it wouldn't be right to skip pointing out that Mike Huckabee — who wants to be President — thinks women who have abortions are just like a million bagillion Hitlers:

"If you felt something incredibly powerful at Auschwitz and Birkenau over the 11 million killed worldwide and the 1.5 million killed on those grounds, cannot we feel something extraordinary about 55 million murdered in our own country in the wombs of their mothers?"

44. Abortion is so horrible that women who are in the process of making the difficult decision to have one should be 'read their rights' like criminals according to 2016 GOP contender Piyush Jindal:

"When officers arrest criminals today, they are read their rights. Now if we're giving criminals their basic rights and they have to be informed of those rights, it seems to me only common sense we would have to do the same thing for women before they make the choice about whether to get an abortion."

45. But do women know, anyway — besides laying back and spreading their legs?

In August 2015, Republican Perryville, MO school board member Mark Germaud shut down (or he thought he did, anyway) fellow member Kathy Carron by letting her know her place — which is apparently the bedroom: *"Kathy, you are just a woman, the only thing you know is laying on your back with your legs in the air splayed."*

This is just a small sampling of the horrific remarks Republicans have made regarding women. It's no surprise, of course, that women are more likely to be Democrats than Republicans. In April, Pew Research Center revealed that women tend to lean Democratic by an overwhelming 52-36 percent. But to those 36 percent of women who insist on voting against their own interest: **Learn more about the candidates to whom you are considering lending your support.**

Republicans may have "binders full of women," but Democrats have the best interests of women at heart. One of the first bills President Obama signed into law, for example, was the Lilly Ledbetter Fair Pay Act of 2009, which allows women to fight back if they are being discriminated against in their pay. The Affordable Care Act provides women preventative care, prevents insurance companies from considering womanhood a pre-existing condition and, last year, President Obama signed two executive orders aimed at narrowing the wage gap between men and women in every area in which he had the power to do so.

The GOP, of course, has fought tooth and nail against pay equality, against a woman's right to choose whether or not she wants to have a child, and against women's rights in general. Remember this in 2016 when you go to the polls.

Author: John PragerJohn Prager is an unfortunate Liberal soul who lives uncomfortably in the middle of a Conservative hellscape. John is the managing editor of Winning Democrats. He moonlights as a counselor at one of Barry Soetoro's FEMA re-education camps and as a HAARP weather control coordinator. John's life's aspiration is to rule the world with an iron fist, or find that sock he's been looking for. Feel free to email him at americanlesionx@gmail.com if you have any questions or comments -- or drop him a line on Twitter or Facebook.

Thanks to John Prager for collecting this information in one place for us at:

http://addictinginfo.org/2015/08/26/these-45-horrible-gop-quotes-show-why-no-woman-should-vote-republican-ever/

This is the most complete list of the incredibly insulting nonsense being spouted by men in 21st century America. I must admit that the sheer ignorance of these statements astonished me. I do not spend a lot of time hanging out with Republican men and I was assuming that educated men, at least, had evolved a bit more than this. The things men have to say about rape alone suggest that we have not "come a long way baby". These guys are still cave men who take what they want and if they have to club a woman over the head to have her, well that's the way God made us and it insures that the human species will survive.

The attack on contraception was so atavistic that it took the whole campaign over-the-top for me. I thought the days of thinking of contraception as mini-abortions were over. But obviously I was very wrong. Not only are contraceptives aborting babies, according to these men, but they are allowing women to enjoy their sexuality which is turning them into sluts and turning our nation into Sodom and Gomorrah.

How can you overturn a Supreme Court decision without going through the Constitutionally-approved process for doing so? The process to overturn is long and arduous and highly unlikely to succeed with over half the population being female and possessed of the right to vote.

During the Obama years the GOP decided to pursue tricky strategies to attack women's health and reproductive rights nonstop. They voted to defund Planned Parenthood, provider of safe, inexpensive abortion to less affluent women, so many times that I cannot even remember the number anymore. They held these votes even though they had already passed laws that said no federal money could be used to pay for abortions. They have forced Planned Parenthood to fight, but also to face the fact that they will probably have to look for all-private funding in the future. So poor women are the losers here, forced to find money to pay for abortions or have an unwanted child because the money cannot be spared. Unwanted children often become problems we all deal with collectively as these children age.

Another technique that has proven quite effective in this "war on women" is to pass TRAP laws (Targeted Regulation of Abortion Providers). TRAP laws require abortion clinics to meet standards that turn them into little hospitals, standards that are far beyond the means of most abortion clinics who have no access to any federal dollars, and are unnecessary for either safety or sanitation reasons.

These laws have only one purpose, to force abortion clinics to close and in the states, like Texas, where such laws have been passed women find they have to travel long distances to get an abortion, something poor women are unlikely to be able to do. In some cases women close to the border go into Mexico to have an abortion and take their chances on clinics that may not have to comply with any regulations. The courts have ruled against some of these attacks, but the clinics have not come back. The technique has been very effective in Republican-controlled states.

Women were quite shocked, I think, to find themselves under verbal and legislative attacks that we felt we had already fought through. Our Mothers spoke of the use of coat hangers as instruments of abortion often enough to lead us to conclude that many women had resorted to this method, which we know led to sometimes unplanned consequences such as the death of the mother, or damage to the fetus. There are abortion stories from the most ancient of days, stories of herbs women could collect and ingest that would rid them of an unwanted pregnancy. Men would be willing to kill a woman who got pregnant inconveniently on occasion. Putting women's health care in their own hands, taking men who often need to express their dominance out of the equation, is key to allowing women to be free citizens of the world. Taking reproductive choices out of women's hands once again is something women will not take lightly and women will have to find ways to keep the independence they have won, because the general direction in which cultures move is forward not backward.

Chapter 6

The Second Amendment

"A well regulated Militia, being necessary to the security of a free State, the right of the people to keep and bear Arms, shall not be infringed."

The Second Amendment was most likely quite definitive in 1789 when the Constitution was ratified. Our young nation had just fought a war with England. They tried to build protections into the Constitution that would allow a fledgling United States to survive against European countries with large armies and navies. So they wrote this Amendment in what seems today to be two different parts.

This Amendment is slippery in part because it has been written backwards. In contemporary composition the part of the sentence after the comma actually would come first and the second comma would then be unnecessary. The construction of the sentence is somewhat archaic which twists a modern brain like a pretzel. Our forefathers say that the people's right to keep and bear arms is not to be infringed upon (by the government) and then they tie that freedom to the necessity of having an army (a Militia).

We know that there were no permanent armed forces in America in those early years. The states collected volunteer soldiers, people who owned farms and businesses or perhaps were lawyers or doctors, furniture makers or silversmiths, even slackers and ruffians and put together armed forces as they were needed to fight in wars or to quell uprisings or to protect their wives and children and their communities from some harm. These temporary soldiers came with their own arms since the new nation did not have a large supply of armaments. Often they even came with their own uniforms and camp equipment. Most early Americans owned a gun anyway since hunting still supplied settlers with meat and there were still hostile conditions at times.

Is this an Amendment whose meaning is somewhat unclear? Republicans say no. Democrats feel that it is perhaps open to some interpretation. This is creating problems in modern America that our forefathers did not foresee. And that inverted grammar does not help.

The National Rifle Association has stepped in to elucidate the Second Amendment for us. In fact, Republicans have pledged allegiance to the NRA. The NRA can make sure that any Republican can have a powerful opponent in a primary election if they have not faithfully fulfilled their pledge to the NRA. This intervention by a private "club" in the governance of America makes things more difficult when it comes to deciding how we want to handle the issue of guns and gun ownership. The NRA is meddling in matters that are Constitutional matters and therefore are the province of our government.

What are the motives of the NRA for standing as a basically immoveable obstacle to rational discussion about guns in America? Well there are various theories. One is that the NRA is actually protecting gun manufacturers and gun businesses. It's working. You don't see our gun manufacturers leaving the country although they might be relocating within our borders.

Another is that the NRA has become the military arm of the Tea Party Republicans who worry that they may have to mount an insurrection against a recalcitrant government that is too big, too powerful, too regulatory, and will not see that Republicans have the right answers for keeping America the number one world power going forward. The Republicans may find that American has arrived at a "Jesus take the wheel" moment. And since Jesus is on their side it won't be hubris to claim that they are just acting for him.

While it is true that there have always been plenty of guns in the hands of American citizens it has also been true that there is plenty of gun violence in our past. Presently, in a more crowded America, gun violence seems to threaten American peace of mind and our national moods more than ever.

Our police have become our domestic army and our community police force. These two goals clash and would seem to be a recipe for disaster. Police departments across America were allowed to buy the war machines that were made to be used in recent wars, the leftovers so to speak. Since police might be fighting terrorists this seemed like a necessary move. But there were no rules. There was nothing to stop police from using equipment designed for waging war as "new toys" to use in more domestic settings like demonstrations and mass shooter situations. It is not that these tools of war have not been very useful in some situations. But when every America potentially could be armed and police are hyperaware of what is unfolding around them escalation is an all too likely response whether called for or not.

How do we stay true to the words of our founders and stop being drowned in grief at all too frequent intervals? How do we make a sensible gun policy when we are not even allowed to discuss the subject without being accused of trampling on the second amendment? How can it be that some of us argue in favor of blind people owning guns, or say yes to those we know to be mentally ill or perhaps allow people on mind-altering medications to own guns?

I guess we must conclude that having the right to bear arms is so important that any price is not too high. National grief be damned.

Mourning family members will not be allowed to interfere. We will instead go nuclear – guns everywhere – open carry everywhere. We have a picture that went viral on the internet of a young man with a semiautomatic rifle slung over his shoulder, dressed in camo, shopping casually in a Walmart.

Mass Shootings

A List of the Deadliest Mass Shootings in Modern US History

1. Pulse Orlando Nightclub in Orlando, Fla. June 12, 2016
2. Virginia Tech in Blacksburg, Va. April 16, 2007
3. Sandy Hook Elementary School in Newtown, Conn. Dec. 14, 2012
4. Luby's Cafeteria in Killeen, Texas (Oct. 16, 1991
5. McDonald's restaurant in San Ysidro, Calif. July 18, 1984
6. University of Texas Tower in Austin, Texas Aug. 1, 1966
7. Columbine High School in Littleton, Colo. April 20, 1999
8. Edmond Post Office in Edmond, Okla. Aug. 20, 1986
9. Inland Regional Center in San Bernardino, Calif. Dec. 2, 2015
10. American Civic Association, Binghamton, NY April 3, 2009
11. Fort Hood in Texas Nov. 5, 2009
12. Washington Navy Yard in Washington, DC Sept. 16, 2013

http://www.npr.org/sections/thetwo-way/2016/06/12/481768384/a-list-of-the-deadliest-mass-shootings-in-u-s-history

It is practically impossible to keep this list up to date. The motivations of the shooters are not always the same. Several of the worst incidents were at the hands of young people, perhaps mentally ill, perhaps not, but certainly young people who felt left out of our culture, who felt alienated and alone and angry.

On December 15, 2012, after the horrendous mass shooting at Sandy Hook Elementary School I wrote this article which I gave the title "Speechless".

I honestly don't know what to say. I am rarely speechless but I just don't understand how we will ever tackle this awful new aspect of life in America. Anyone, it seems, can walk into any public place in America toting automatic and semi-automatic guns and just open fire. Of course, killing 5-year-olds has to be a new low. How does someone talk himself into doing something like this? What reasons could you give yourself that would allow a grown man to open fire on children? We have watched children dying in Syria, or Israel, or Palestine, or Africa and have found this profoundly incomprehensible even in a time of war. But we are not at war. How senseless these mass murders are!

Yet we cannot conceive of a set of steps that we could follow to prevent other acts like this. We don't know how to predict who will commit these heinous and cowardly acts. Is such an act a manifestation of hate, or anger, or depression, or delusion? Does each act represent a unique emotional state? Either we have to take a more controlled approach to mental illness or we have to think about gun control. Why wouldn't we want to do both? If we can't prevent this will we eventually harden our hearts to such random violence? That would be bad. There is little comfort we can offer parents who will not get to watch their child grow up and who will have to live with such a seemingly pointless death.

Yes we will pray. We will pray that there is a heaven for these innocent children. We will pray that the parents find peace and that their lives eventually offer them some solace to make up for this pain. We will pray that America outgrows this particular type of crime and we will pray that we learn to parent in ways that produce well-adjusted children, adolescents and adults. We will pray that we learn better ways to identify and help people who are mentally ill. We will pray that it is done. Enough! And we will mourn.

http://thearmchairobserver.com/speechless/ 12/15/12

After the shocking killings at a Bible study group in Charleston, SC, I wrote this article with the title "Through Our Tears".

I could not write about the sad, sad killings in Charleston, SC right away because I wanted to get some perspective first (as if this short amount of time could help). I am not sure why this particular mass shooting has hit me so hard but I can't think about it without crying. I guess I was in shock when the twenty-six beautiful children were shot in Newtown. I mourned but it did not bring tears to my eyes or leave this thickness in my throat. Perhaps it is the weight of all these deadly incidents piling up that makes this time so hard. Perhaps it is the innocence of nine American people of African Descent in a church studying a Bible and accepting a young man of Caucasian Descent into their midst. Maybe it is because he sat with them for an hour and then killed them. How could he carry out his twisted "mission" once he knew these people personally? I don't understand how America got here or how we will move away from this place, or even if we can stop hate now.

We cannot bring these lovely people back. I did not know them but their survivors speak so highly of them and the things the relatives said to that boy/man at his arraignment were things I don't think I ever could have said, so I just know that these were good people.

We have to, have to, try to figure out how to raise these alienated young people that American seems to have homegrown in greater numbers than previously over the past three or four decades. We have to figure out how to give them the connectedness they need, offer them more love and acceptance, and find tasks for them that make them feel useful. Our churches are not as central to our lives as they once were. Our families are sometimes failing to offer the support children need as they grow and mature. Our mental health system turned away from one-on-one therapy to medications that have not proven to be as efficacious as they were first believed to be, often because side effects lead people to stop medicating, or are even to misuse them to the point of unhealthy addiction. Our schools are left to handle children who are well-adjusted and those who are not with very little help from anyone. Those who are not well-adjusted leave school far too early because they can see that the schools haven't the slightest idea about how to help them turn their lives around.

Then we have the divided nature of our nation right now. We have to look at those in the media who have been venting their anger/hate about minorities and about the poor; who have been pretending that their attitude towards guns is about freedom and the Second Amendment when they have almost been, have walked the line past, talking about revolution and secession because they believe their brand of the American way of life is being governed out of existence. Folks who spew hate 24/7 must bear some responsibility for giving angry "misfits" a script to follow. I do believe in free speech. Perhaps we just don't need quite so much of it and it doesn't always have to sound quite so passionate about every little imagined slight.

We also have to look at the gang culture in our cities which gives young people an alternative to belong to an organization, but belonging to this particular organization puts them at odds with the rest of society, turns them into criminals, and finally delivers them to a life in prison where they are fed and clothed, and sometimes educated, but where they, all too often, are initiated into a life that puts them outside the hopefully more satisfying and certainly more peaceful arc of a productive mainstream life.

Perhaps it is time to haul out that old idea of two years of community service for our kids who opt out of college or training programs. Perhaps our mental health system needs another overhaul where we take some of the freedom to choose or not choose medication away from the mentally ill until we can find a genetic way out of this difficult-to-live-with mental wiring. Or we must harden our hearts and grieve as we go and live in fear that we also might be in the right place at the wrong time.

http://thearmchairobserver.com/through-our-tears/ 6/21/15

Flirting with Insurrection

At times it has felt that the south was going to "rise again", except the epicenter of this uprising looked like it might be located in Texas. Texas is the home of Ted Cruz, child of a Cuban who fled Cuba because he possibly would have been killed or imprisoned by the Castro's, child of an American woman who moved to Canada and changed her citizenship. Ted Cruz of the cynical smarmy smile that never quite reaches his eyes, Congressional disrupter, fomenter of government shutdowns. I see Ted Cruz's hand in the spirit of insurrection surfacing in red states. He owes his rise to the Tea Party and there is nothing the Tea Party loves as much as making up nightmares to scare themselves and the rest of the American people who like their angry, we're-being-cheated politics.

So we have seen a few eruptions of this insurrectionist meme that has run throughout the Obama years as a minor part of the major obstructionist agenda that the Republicans have hurled against this man. We do not know for sure if they are angrier that a Democrat has the "con" or that he is an American of African Descent. They tried to delegitimize his presidency by claiming that he was actually a Kenyan and that he was a Muslim (there are no religious requirements for Presidents).

I call many of the moves that Ted Cruz and his band of Tea Partiers made in Washington insurrectionist in nature. Ted Cruz studied Constitutional Law at Harvard. He is obsessed with the American Constitution and if he could get his hands on it he might change our interpretation and implementation of this document that underlies our entire nation in ways that would profoundly change America itself. Many feel it is his dearest desire to get on the Supreme Court and stay there for the rest of his life so that he can bring his brand of Evangelical Christianity and Fundamentalism to bear of the moral underpinnings of our nation. It is my dearest desire to make sure that this man is never allowed to realize his fondest dreams.

Here is a man who says he reveres our US Constitution and yet he acts like a revolutionary who will overthrow governance as we know it. He says he is worried about our fiscal soundness as a nation and that he is willing to shut down our government and cost us all millions of dollars to make a point that many economists do not even believe is accurate. He is a troublemaker offering us snide expressions and a smug, arrogant manner. I guess you get the picture. I don't think much of Ted Cruz.

I am sad to see the South is still lost in dreams of glory about the Confederacy. I am also sorry about the *posse comitatus* laws (which I learned about from Rachel Maddow) which gave so much power back to local sheriffs during the Reconstruction Era in the South that it allowed the South to hold on to the illusions that the rise of the Confederacy and victory for the South was still possible. The power residing in local sheriffs, that supposedly trumps the power of the Federal government, is also very attractive to those folks with a strong independent streak like the people we see in states that are to the West of the original thirteen colonies.

One of the clearest avatars of this contempt for Federal authority popped up unexpectedly one day in the news when armed men from Washington showed up to force a rancher, Cliven Bundy, to stop grazing his cattle on Federal land or to pay the fees that other ranchers had to pay. They had tried to make their point in more peaceful ways before they made this probably ill-advised and armed ultimatum. It did not go well. We watched armed and independent militias show up ready to shoot back at the Federal marshals. The government backed down before events could reach a point of no return but it shocked me, and many other Americans. It became clear how divided we are as Americans, in front of their TV's, took sides.

I wrote about Cliven Bundy and the implications of that strange confrontation on 4/16/14 (just to remind us of when these events took place) in an article entitled "Bizarro America or 'Release the Kracken'"

Cliven Bundy is a rancher in Nevada. I first read about him in the **Daily Kos** and then saw a more detailed story on *All In with Chris Hayes* on **MSNBC**. He has been grazing his cattle on federal land for about 20 years. Ranchers are allowed to let their stock graze federal land but ranchers pay a fee for this right. All of the other Nevada ranchers have kept up with their fees but not Cliven Bundy. He says he does not recognize the federal government (of the United States of America) which is a very interesting belief, especially when you now owe the federal government and the American people about $1 million dollars.

The government, having tried unsuccessfully to collect the fees owed, started collecting Bundy's cattle in corrals they had built and they were preparing to truck his cattle to market and sell them so they could apply the proceeds against Bundy's debt. Bundy had other ideas and he had a large group of family and friends, sort of militia-type friends, who came, well-armed, to join the fray. So we have US Bureau of Land Use and Management Rangers lined up on one side of a ragged line across an interstate and we have Bundy's "army" lined up across from them. A few pushes and lots of angry words ensue. The US Rangers decide that it is not a good day to die and, fortunately, they back off before anyone does. But now we have the impromptu militia winning the battle and freeing the cattle – more federal bucks down the drain. What will the next move be for the feds? Bundy warns the county sheriffs to arm themselves as they are the only authority he accepts (I'm guessing marginally). No one leaves happy.

…

Mr. Bundy is lawless in a way that scares me because he does not see himself as lawless. He believes that he is a free American with free speech (free thought) and guns who must defend what he believes even though it is unconstitutional and illegal, and will lead us into anarchy if everyone starts to behave in this way. However if I owed the federal government one million dollars I might try to tough it out in the manner of Mr. Bundy, especially if I knew I had support. We can hope that the government gets creative and finds a nonviolent way to make its point and bring this situation to a quick end. But the larger problem of the anger that has been fomented in Americans will still remain and we need a really good lightning rod to deflect all that explosive energy and ground it.

Is all this bizarre enough for you? It gives me the shivers.

http://thearmchairobserver.com/bizarro-america-or-release-kraken/ 4/16/14

In fact I have written about guns in America many times because this topic has bubbled up frequently in the American conversation, and usually we give it a bit of our attention each time that violence comes up in our news feed. However we soon accept that there is still no way such a conversation can turn into constructive action. We remain under the thumb of the NRA, their many unshakeable members, and their allies in the Republican Party.

I cannot leave this topic without taking us back to Texas because of the things I have said about this possibly most insurrectionist state of all. If we couldn't start a shoot-out with Cliven Bundy (which did eventually come to pass with his son) then perhaps we could start a war by passing around a really off-the-wall conspiracy theory. When the US government approached the date of some mock war exercises they had planned to conduct in Texas people began to talk about the operation as an actual attack that our government intended to begin against Texas. They said that the operation would be called Jade Helm and that certain Walmart stores were being prepared as prisons for those captured during this attack. What the government planned to do with these prisoners is unclear to me.

However wacky stuff like this sounds it is a symptom of an underlying unease some Americans have about their own Federal government. This paranoia has obviously been stoked by someone. It could not have been arrived at spontaneously by so many people all at the same time. I don't really believe in group hallucinations. Someone convinced Texans that this was a real operation meant to subdue a rebellious Texas. I blame Tea Party Talk Radio and Fox News. You may place the blame elsewhere. I do worry that loose conspiracy talk like this could cause panic and precipitate a war that would end America forever. Is that where we are headed with all these guns and all this flirting with insurrection?

On May 10, 2015 I wrote "Texas, We Think You Need an Intervention, We Think You Need Therapy"

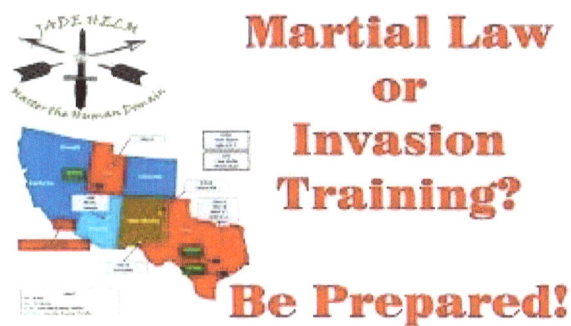

Texas, you big baby! You're like a dysfunctional child in a big family, a demanding child, always throwing tantrums. I suppose when you are the biggest state you tend to throw your weight around but you would get your own way more often if you didn't always demand changes to the very things that are accepted as the law of the land in most other states. You are never dull, I will give you that, but you're like this wild child that we wish we could give a long time out. You are like a juvenile delinquent who breaks all the rules just to prove that you are not bound by them. You want us to understand that you make your own rules and will never accept majority rule when you don't agree with the majority.

Since you get your religion all mixed up in this perhaps you are more like the preacher's son, rebellious but also devout. You are Fundamentalist in your religion (or perhaps Catholic), Fundamentalist in your interpretation of the US

Constitution, and you are good ole boys with pickups and beer, but you also want America to stay white, Christian, English speaking, heterosexual, and the number one Superpower feared and respected around the globe. Some of these goals of yours are totally unrealistic (and not at all civil).

We have spent an inordinate amount of time paying attention to your concerns. You have complained that there is massive voter fraud and that we must tighten up voting by requiring voter ID's. You have shown no sympathy for American citizens who might find it difficult to access the documents necessary to acquire such an ID. You don't care if these voter are disenfranchised as a result of your obsession with your unsupported paranoia about illegal voters. Since Texas prides itself on being a "red" state you feel that it is a bonus if most of the votes you suppress are from people who will likely vote for Democrats.

You circumvent federal law which makes abortion legal and you have found ways to pack Texas State government with Evangelicals who cannot stay out of women's reproductive lives, because, the Bible. Women with money are not much affected by this because they can afford to travel to have an abortion although it is an inconvenience. But the proliferation of TRAP laws which pass stringent rules for abortion clinics that are impossible for them to comply with have caused clinics to close all over Texas, especially in Western Texas thus forcing poor women, who cannot travel, to have unwanted children, to self-abort, or to perhaps cross over into Mexico for an abortion at their peril.

Not once have you tried to pass any laws that would help women financially while carrying a child to term against their better inclinations. Not once have you tried to pass laws that would help a women take a blameless hiatus in a career in order to give birth. And you also have not set up any alternative system to help the children who might be born to women who were in no position to raise them. Getting mixed up in women's business because you feel you occupy a moral high road is another of the things you do, Texas, that drive the rest of us to keep a jaundiced eye on your rebellious ways.

We have long heard of your prickly fears that the Federal government is too powerful; that your state, and in fact all states need more autonomy and less helicoptering by Washington, a parent so overprotective as to be almost actually teetering on the edge of totalitarianism. (Gasp)

You whine that America wants to take away all your guns in order to prevent America from passing the teensiest laws regulating gun registration or ownership. You encourage the formation of belligerent, intimidating militias seemingly because you admire eccentrics. Yes the Constitution allows us to form militias, but in trying to protect your state from the big, bad federal government these folks are actually fomenting trouble with the big, bad feds.

Maybe you are all true paranoids or maybe you have learned that America will back off and give you space if they think you will explode under the slightest pressure. This allows you to get away with just about anything and once again you have our undivided attention. You have outdone yourselves this time. We can only shake our heads in wonder. Secret tunnels connecting Walmart stores as part of a conspiracy to turn US military exercises into a war on Texas? If we are going to go to war with Texas it looks like we should send in the shrinks, not the tanks. It is very telling that your Governor and Congressional leaders act like these conspiracy theories are real rather than groundless nonsense.

http://thearmchairobserver.com/texas-this-is-intervention-we-think-you/ 5/10/15

We are actually not allowed to discuss what our forefathers meant by the Second Amendment because the Tea Party and the Republican Party have become the guardians of a particular interpretation of that amendment and the rest of us are soundly snubbed and overruled if we want to change anything about what our founders meant with their antique sentence structure. In reality the NRA now owns the Second Amendment of the US Constitution. All the rest of us can do is mourn when we must and wait out the zeitgeist of the moment.

Here is a list of the many times I have written about guns in the past five years and the topic has come up in the media many more times than this"

http://thearmchairobserver.com/randomness/ 1/10/11

http://thearmchairobserver.com/our-guns/ 1/11/11

http://thearmchairobserver.com/lock-up-your-guns/ 3/1/12

http://thearmchairobserver.com/trayvon-martin-i-dont-understand/ 3/30/12

http://thearmchairobserver.com/we-need-new-approach-to-mental-illness/ 7/21/12

http://thearmchairobserver.com/speechless/ 12/15/12

http://thearmchairobserver.com/guns-and-twinkies/ 4/9/13

http://thearmchairobserver.com/the-paradox-of-our-second-amendmen/ 7/16/13

http://thearmchairobserver.com/is-crazy-man-defending-guns-in-america/ 9/18/13

http://thearmchairobserver.com/bizarro-america-or-release-kraken/ 4/16/14

http://thearmchairobserver.com/guns-everywhere-waiting-out-fanatics/ 6/9/14

http://thearmchairobserver.com/the-hatefear-loopand-guns/ 8/17/14

http://thearmchairobserver.com/solving-our-policing-dilemmas/ 12/28/14

http://thearmchairobserver.com/texas-this-is-intervention-we-think-you/ 5/10/15

http://thearmchairobserver.com/through-our-tears/ 6/21/15

http://thearmchairobserver.com/the-roots-of-gun-culture/ 9/7/15

http://thearmchairobserver.com/guns-everywhere-mistakes-will-be-made/ 12/6/15

Chapter 7

The 15th Amendment – Voter Suppression and the Supreme Court

1) The right of citizens of the United States to vote shall not be denied or abridged by the United States or any state on account of race, color, or previous condition of servitude.

2) The Congress shall have power to enforce this article by appropriate legislation.

Wikipedia gives us the following description of the Voting Rights Act which was added to the body of law about voting in America in 1965. It was necessary because many states kept devising new voting requirements and tests to prevent minorities from voting. It adds to the body of law and tradition that has become a part of the US Constitution.

Wikipedia says, "The **Voting Rights Act of 1965** is a landmark piece of <u>federal</u> <u>legislation</u> in the <u>United States</u> that prohibits racial discrimination in <u>voting</u>. It was signed into law by <u>President</u> <u>Lyndon B. Johnson</u> during the height of the <u>Civil Rights Movement</u> on August 6, 1965, and <u>Congress</u> later amended the Act five times to expand its protections. Designed to enforce the <u>voting rights</u> guaranteed by the <u>Fourteenth</u> and <u>Fifteenth Amendments</u> to the <u>United States Constitution</u>, the Act secured voting rights for <u>racial minorities</u> throughout the country, especially in the <u>South</u>.

The Act contains numerous provisions that regulate election administration. The Act's "general provisions" provide nationwide protections for voting rights. Section 2 is a general provision that prohibits every <u>state</u> and <u>local government</u> from imposing any voting law that results in discrimination against racial or language minorities. Other general provisions specifically outlaw <u>literacy tests</u> and similar devices that were historically used to disenfranchise racial minorities.

The Act also contains "special provisions" that apply to only certain jurisdictions. A core special provision is the Section 5 preclearance requirement, which prohibits certain jurisdictions from implementing any change affecting voting without receiving preapproval from the <u>U.S. Attorney General</u> or the <u>U.S. District Court for D.C.</u> that the change does not discriminate against protected minorities. Another special provision requires jurisdictions containing significant language minority populations to provide underline bilingual ballots and other election materials.

Section 5 and most other special provisions apply to jurisdictions encompassed by the "coverage formula" prescribed in Section 4(b). The coverage formula was originally designed to encompass jurisdictions that engaged in egregious voting discrimination in 1965, and Congress updated the formula in 1970 and 1975. In _Shelby County v. Holder_ (2013), the U.S. Supreme Court struck down the coverage formula as unconstitutional, reasoning that it was no longer responsive to current conditions. The Court did not strike down Section 5, but without a coverage formula, Section 5 is unenforceable.

In the 1950s, the Civil Rights Movement increased pressure on the federal government to protect the voting rights of racial minorities. In 1957, Congress passed the first civil rights legislation since Reconstruction: the Civil Rights Act of 1957. This legislation authorized the Attorney General to sue for injunctive relief on behalf of persons whose Fifteenth Amendment rights were deprived, created the Civil Rights Division within the Department of Justice to enforce civil rights through litigation, and created the Commission on Civil Rights to investigate voting rights deprivations. Further protections were enacted in the Civil Rights Act of 1960, which allowed federal courts to appoint referees to conduct voter registration in jurisdictions that engaged in voting discrimination against racial minorities.

Congress responded to rampant discrimination against racial minorities in public accommodations and government services by passing the Civil Rights Act of 1964.

...

In the wake of the events in Selma, President Johnson, addressing a televised joint session of Congress on March 15, called on legislators to enact expansive voting rights legislation. He concluded his speech with the words "we shall overcome", a major theme of the Civil Rights Movement. The legislation that Johnson referred to was the Voting Rights Act of 1965, which was introduced in Congress two days later while civil rights leaders, now under the protection of federal troops, led a march of 25,000 people from Selma to Montgomery.

When determining whether a jurisdiction's election law violates this general prohibition, courts have relied on factors enumerated in the Senate Judiciary Committee report associated with the 1982 amendments ("Senate Factors"), including:

1. The history of official discrimination in the jurisdiction that affects the right to vote;
2. The degree to which voting in the jurisdiction is racially polarized;
3. The extent of the jurisdiction's use of majority vote requirements, unusually large electoral districts, prohibitions on bullet voting, and other devices that tend to enhance the opportunity for voting discrimination;
4. Whether minority candidates are denied access to the jurisdiction's candidate slating processes, if any;
5. The extent to which the jurisdiction's minorities are discriminated against in socioeconomic areas, such as education, employment, and health;
6. Whether overt or subtle racial appeals in campaigns exist;
7. The extent to which minority candidates have won elections;

8. The degree that elected officials are unresponsive to the concerns of the minority group; and

9. Whether the policy justification for the challenged law is tenuous.

The report indicates not all or a majority of these factors need to exist for an electoral device to result in discrimination, and it also indicates that this list is not exhaustive, allowing courts to consider additional evidence at their discretion.

…

Section 5 requires that covered jurisdictions receive federal approval, known as "preclearance", before implementing changes to their election laws."

(I have changed the links (underlined) from blue ink to black and I have deleted the attributions, but they are still available in Wikipedia.)

In The Armchair Observer I wrote:

Freedom Grudgingly Granted

I am not a person of color, unless you like the color of raw chicken skin (I'm a bit short on pigmentation) so I should really mind my own campfire and leave this topic alone. However, when you believe, as I do, that everything and everyone is interconnected then you tend to take liberties with boundaries, as in the sense that when you look at earth from space the only boundaries you see are geological.

I am not talking about some hippie-dippy dabbling in Eastern philosophy kind of interconnectedness. I am talking about the-ripples-from a-pebble-dropped-in-water, you-and-I-breathe-the-same- air, drink-the-same-water, share-the-same-food-requirements, and fall-prey-to-the-same-diseases kind of interconnectedness. While the effects we have on each other were not quite so obvious or significant when the earth was less populated, now that we are 7 billion strong, headed for 9 billion real soon, we are beginning to experience our interconnectedness daily and not always in good ways.

So pardon me as I venture into a space that really isn't mine, because I don't like injustice and I think cultures should champion fairness. Certain things are true about the lives of many (although perhaps not all) Americans of African descent which testify to a lack of justice and fairness that needs to be set right if our grand experiment in Democracy is to continue. That very fact, that we have not lived up to our own creed is weighing on us and is negatively affecting our ability to act as a viable example to the rest of the globe about what is possible.

I know we are just as flawed as any other humans when considered as individuals. This is why people form societies – with the hope that collectively we will be able to overcome some of our individual flaws. Often our human flaws only get magnified because power and wealth are so corrupting but, in our Democracy, answering to more humble humans is supposed to keep the corruption in check. What we have done to Americans of African descent in America is a shameful example of what happens when justice and fairness have been circumvented.

Yes, we had a Civil War and the slaves were freed. But they certainly did not go from freedom to inclusion in any quick hurry. Yes, the Civil Rights Movement, won by brave people who bucked hatred and exclusion, won by people who spoke out against being bullied into a social position that was still submissive, a movement won by people who risked their very lives to insist on a greater share of respect and a greater share in the rights and privileges that all white people enjoyed, did result in a somewhat greater measure of freedom for African Americans. Yes, the Civil Rights Act of 1964 was signed and many white Americans grudgingly accepted things like voting rights and the rights of Black Americans to share public spaces.

Hatred, however, is very sneaky and it finds ways to skirt laws. Many in our society have found nasty ways to show how truly unhappy they were about sharing rights equally with African Americans, and these same haters developed ways to use real estate to keep Americans of African descent from intermingling with white folks, unless they were wealthy enough or well-educated enough to find their way around the secret exclusionary practices used by citizens to manipulate the sale of real estate. Now we complain about neighborhoods populated almost exclusively by Americans of African descent, neighborhoods we created by allowing unfair real estate practices. We blame the victims so to speak.

Not only do we complain about so-called black neighborhoods (which we created) but we complain when the residents of these neighborhoods show enough zest for life that they turn around and create their own colorful and compelling culture.

Well I say we need to get a grip – if you keep a group separate and you show a reluctance to let African Americans live amongst you then you must not be surprised when they make a culture that gets along without you.

We cannot let the situation remain as it currently exists. We don't seem able to let African American people live in peace. It is not healthy to have a society within a society for one thing. Although we have managed this exact configuration with Native Americans who supposedly have sovereignty, but still are subject to the laws that govern America to some extent, this has always been, and still is, an awkward arrangement.

Americans of African descent are suffering due to their isolation. They are not buying into the education their children need to get good jobs. They are being arrested and imprisoned in numbers that are way too high. Although their culture is thriving in some respects, it is being artificially stunted in others. We are becoming, more and more, two separate societies, one with the power to punish, one with only the power to disrupt. Disruption shows strength, but it shuts down the opportunities to be successful within the structure of the larger society. All this has been aggravated by the arc of the American economy. As soon as Black Americans started to get good jobs, the factories left America. As soon as they got houses (a great big scam on them anyway) the housing bubble burst.

To continue down the paths of separation that we have been on will only lead to more of what we already abhor and to the failure of our great experiment in equality and justice for all. Everyone will lose.

I can see where we are headed but I can't see how to build a route out of a more and more divided future. I know I always say that according to our DNA we are all the same, but cultural differences are very real and have been intensified by separation. I felt proud when Obama reminded us that we are not a Black America and a White American or a Red State and Blue State America; we are the United States of America!

I truly believe that if we elect Republicans in 2016 we stop any conversation about these matters in their tracks and we go our separate ways probably for as long as we all shall live. And once we snip the social safety net and send all the jobs away we will no longer have any Americans of African descent because they will have to form their own country somewhere on land that is currently American land in order to survive. Maybe they will want to live in the Southern US because the economy there is doing somewhat better than elsewhere and they have ties to the area. Perhaps they will want Detroit and Chicago and that will make Wisconsin look attractive also. Perhaps I'm just pulling your chain, but maybe not.

It is clear that we are making tomorrow's Black History today and we need to try to write a much happier chapter than the one we have been writing.

http://thearmchairobserver.com/freedom-grudgingly-granted-black/

In 2014 parts the Civil Rights Act and the Voting Rights Act turned 50 years old. Although this is an occasion well worth celebrating and John Lewis, who was there at the beginning, was there to mark the event, things were a bit subdued. The joy we all should have felt was muffled by the revelations of the racism we have known about but which have become clearer in the two terms of our first President who is an American of African Descent. We did not just dredge up the victory of the Civil Rights Act but all the vitriol that preceded it. All of the reluctance of white America to accept the freedoms won by black folks in the Civil War - all of the marches, the dogs, the firehoses, the sorrow of innocents killed, and the meanness of whites who did not plan to ever treat their former slaves as equals.

When we speak of the 1960's we speak of a time that is a century after the Civil War, but the gall and the bile of the losers has been kept alive by white Americans, especially some Southern white Americans. We know about the lynching. We know about the terror in the night – the spectacle of men in white gowns and hoods burning crosses on people's lawns. We know about the humiliation of devising tests to use at the polls that black voters would not be able to pass. We know that even now, even 150 years after the Civil War we have not put racism to rest. It is America's collective shame.

It was not enough to pass laws about the rights of black people to vote once. These laws have had to be toughened through several different incarnations. We finally had a version that was working. We had a version which outlawed racial gerrymandering and required states who had broken voting laws in the past to obtain preclearance before any new voting laws were enacted. Giving people early voting and more days to vote and more polling places was bringing more black folks out to vote.

Until now, at the 50th anniversary of the voting rights act, a Supreme Court, stacked to lean right, decided that they would do away with the criteria for setting preclearance rules and states could now change their election laws without asking the courts first. The moment they removed this protection from the law, before the proverbial ink was even dry, Republican controlled states began passing laws to suppress the votes of minorities. They claimed that they were suppressing the votes of Democrats, which is hardly more laudable, but since the minorities they targeted tended to vote for Democrats most of the time their claims made it hard to prove that the changes were signs that the old racism was back. Republicans have argued that they are concerned about voting fraud although there is little proof that voting fraud exists in America beyond about 34 indeterminate cases. Since raising fear levels about voter fraud has not been very effective, since they can't prove voter fraud at home, and because Republicans want to win the Presidency so badly, their newest claim is that our polls have been hacked by foreign nations. If Republicans don't win the Presidency will they try to invalidate the 2016 election?

You can read about the Supreme Court decision in more detail here:

http://www.nytimes.com/2013/06/26/us/supreme-court-ruling.html?_r=0

The following information is from an article posted to prospect.org with the title *Voter Suppression, How Bad? (Pretty Bad)*

For the first time in decades, voters in nearly half the country will find it harder to cast a ballot in the upcoming elections. Voters in 22 states will face tougher rules than in the last midterms. In 15 states, 2014 is slated to be the first major election with new voting restrictions in place.

These changes are the product of a concerted push to restrict voting by legislative majorities that swept into office in 2010. They represent a sharp reversal for a country whose historical trajectory has been to expand voting rights and make the process more convenient and accessible.

…

Partisanship plays a key role. Of the 22 states with new restrictions, 18 passed them through entirely Republican-controlled bodies. A study by social scientists Keith Bentele and Erin O'Brien of the University of Massachusetts Boston found that restrictions were more likely to pass "as the proportion of Republicans in the legislature increased or when a Republican governor was elected." After Republicans took over state houses and governorships in 2010, voting restrictions typically followed party lines.

Race has been a significant factor. In 2008, voter participation among African Americans and certain other groups surged. Then came backlash. The more a state saw increases in minority and low-income voter turnout, the more likely it was to push laws cutting back on voting rights, according to the University of Massachusetts study. The Brennan Center for Justice likewise found that of the 11 states with the highest African American turnout in 2008, seven passed laws making it harder to vote. Of the 12 states with the largest Hispanic population growth in the 2010 Census, nine have new restrictions in place. And of the 15 states that used to be monitored closely under the Voting Rights Act because of a history of racial discrimination in elections, nine passed new restrictions.

…

The number and complexity of new voting restrictions across the country are staggering. As Yale Law Professor Heather Gerken put it, "It's a death-by-a-thousand-cuts strategy."

The data: (summarized)

Voter ID Laws: only 2 states had voter ID laws before 2011

9 states have passed strict new ID laws since 2011:

Alabama, Arkansas, Kansas, Mississippi, North Carolina, Tennessee, Texas, Virginia, Wisconsin

Making it Harder to Register to vote – 10 states:

Curbing voter registration drives:

Florida, Illinois, Texas, Virginia

Proof of citizenship required:

Alabama, Kansas, Tennessee, and at one time Arizona

A law that makes it harder for people who move to stay registered:

Wisconsin

Eliminating same day registration:

Nebraska, North Carolina

Curbs on restoring rights to people with past convictions:

Florida, Iowa, South Dakota

Key states to watch:

North Carolina (more voting restrictions than any other state)

Wisconsin

Kansas

Arizona

Florida

Ohio

Arkansas

http://prospect.org/article/22-states-wave-new-voting-restrictions-threatens-shift-outcomes-tight-races

A few other sources:

https://thinkprogress.org/study-finds-republican-voter-suppression-is-even-more-effective-than-you-think-3b2562ae2f52#.ranccogc1

http://takingnote.blogs.nytimes.com/2016/05/20/the-republicans-obsession-with-voter-suppression/

http://www.huffingtonpost.com/john-wellington-ennis/confronting-voter-suppres_b_9812612.html

Sources with charts and other graphics:

http://www.vox.com/2015/8/6/9107183/voting-rights-map-chart

https://www.americanprogress.org/wp-content/uploads/issues/2012/04/pdf/voter_supression.pdf

http://www.brennancenter.org/analysis/state-voting-2014

These attacks on voting rights are particularly concerning because voting has always showed who was a valued citizen and who did not get to put a finger on the scale in an election. When the Constitution was ratified not everyone could vote. You can still read that section of the document but it has been heavily modified.

We know that many colonists were slave owners. Slaves were counted as 3/5 of a person, but only to establish the population of a state in order to determine the number of representatives elected to the House of Representatives. Women, of course, were disenfranchised by the rules of society. Once women won the vote there were no humiliating tests applied to white women, although black women were sometimes harassed and due to voter ID requirements some older black women are being harassed once again.

It makes little sense in a society where everyone is supposedly equal, at least under the law, for anyone to find it difficult to vote in these days of the 21st century. It is frustrating to watch the GOP conducting voter suppression campaigns, to see that the courts are slow to interfere, and to see these actions affecting the possible outcome of a Presidential election. It is even more frustrating if you have been watched the Republicans trying to skew elections and block Democrats from pursuing their agenda since Obama took office.

Our Constitution gives us no advice about what to do in situations like this. There are no designated referees in our government. No one, except the courts, says "you can't do that" and if a party has packed the courts then that doesn't happen. The people should be the referees, voting out the offenders in the next election but because of the

- extreme gerrymandering of urban districts
- the voter suppression that closes polling places making it difficult for some to get to the polls,
- laws passed that say that college students must vote in their home districts even though they are at school when elections happen
- all of the money in elections, all the PAC's and "dark money"
- all the state governments that the GOP has managed to capture
- the power of Talk Radio and Fox News on the right to disseminate propaganda and basically brainwash voters to think they want things that are actually against their best interests,
- because incumbents usually win these day

because of all these things and more our Constitution cannot help us in 2016. Because of all these things and more I have accused the Republicans of sedition more than once since 2008 and I have warned that we are in the middle of an attempt at a bloodless coup. Democrats seem to believe that even though they cannot hold onto the Legislative branch right now they will be able to hold on to the Presidency which will help liberals hold on to the courts, but I am worried because the Republican assault on our Constitution and our elections seems so well-planned and well-financed. I cannot tell if Donald Trump will actually, in some mad way, help them win the office they have manipulated and disrupted to win or if he will put the kibosh on all their strategizing and finagling. Clearly if we elect a Democrat our nation will continue down familiar paths. If we don't our Constitution and our nation may be changed beyond recognition.

In case you think that this is old news you will want to check out this article about voter ID's in Wisconsin, published in The Nation on September 29, 2016 by Ari Berman.

https://www.thenation.com/article/wisconsin-is-systematically-failing-to-provide-the-photo-ids-required-to-vote-in-november/

The state of Wisconsin just began requiring that voters needed a certified ID in order to vote in November. Many of the people who do not have a way to get a certified ID are Americans of African Descent. These folks were told that if they went to the Wisconsin DMV they could get a voting certified ID in six days. When they got to the DMV the agency, for the most part, knew nothing about this and said that the ID's would take about 8 weeks. This would mean that these citizens would not be able to vote in the 2016 elections. This will eventually be declared unconstitutional, I believe, but it will serve the purpose of suppressing voters who don't usually vote Republican.

Conclusions

I know that not everyone draws the same conclusions when they look at the facts included in this book but perhaps there are many Americans who have not seen all the evidence summarized in one place. When they see it all together the evidence may be more compelling. This evidence suggests that the Republicans have a strategy, a complex strategy, which allows them to attack our Constitution in its current incarnation, and our election laws, with the end goal of controlling all branches of the United States government.

They are trying to make our Constitution a partisan instrument that favors the agenda of the Republican Party. They may honestly feel that our government has become too liberal, that we have wandered away from the intentions of our forefathers and that they mean only to reset the Constitution in a purer form. Thankfully they do not seem interested in restoring the sections that deal with the mind-bending ways in which our forefathers justified owning slaves and treating people as if they were things.

By ignoring the entire body of law and tradition that trails along with our Constitution, by arguing that we need to go back to the original document and take a more fundamentalist view when interpreting what our forefathers wrote the Constitution and the nation could be brought closer in line with Conservative views which more proper, more correct and more likely to keep America prosperous and strong than the liberal way which is causing America to lose its ascendency among the nations of the world.

Republicans argue that trying to create a society that says people are equal instead of a society that allows people to strive to be their best is destroying our nation. We are basically offering pearls to swine, or tax dollar to deadbeats, whichever language you prefer. They want to change the balance of power between the Federal government and the states so that Conservative states can run their business as they believe it should be run. They want to adopt a sort of "tough love" approach to governing that would not waste tax dollars on those who will not strive or show a strong work ethic; who will not do whatever is necessary to care for themselves and their loved ones rather than expecting the government to provide assistance. They feel that the government is now taking the place of all the communal organizations that people once belonged to, clubs that provided services to the truly unfortunate. And they say the government can no longer afford to do this.

However, the people can see how much money some people have managed to funnel into their own bank accounts. We have seen the data. We know that 20% of the people own a much wealth as the other 80% of us. We know about the extreme wealth concentrated in the top 1%, even the top .1%. They have to use underhanded, nearly unconstitutional methods to obtain their ends because we can all see that they have managed to stack the deck in favor of those with money. They do not necessarily have employees in America anymore. They want to cut us loose to sink or swim on our own. Climb out of the pack and show us what you've got they challenge, except this is not 1890 and we are in a transitional age and it is not so easy to climb out of the pack at this particular moment.

Everything has become either a Conservative right wing policy or a Liberal left wing policy but the right wing is winning the tug of war right now. They control 32 state governments either wholly or partially enough to be able to set policy in these "red" states. They have rigged voting districts to suppress the votes of Democrats. They have put actual voter suppression laws in place which are unconstitutional but probably cannot be invalidated before the 2016 election. These laws also are intended to lower votes for Democrats. They have made it possible for rich donors to put as much money into elections as they would like. It you have a local politician running for office whose ads look a bit too slick for local politics then you can bet that national PAC's are trying to buy a positive outcome for their side in the election and that the other party will have to retaliate.

Conservatives have been tinkering with our Constitution, trying to reboot it to an earlier age and then acting as if they have a direct line to what our forefathers meant in some of the more open ended sections of the Constitution. They are trying to turn our Constitution into a document that backs up their partisan views. They are making this key document a Republican Constitution rather than a United States Constitution. They are almost there. The deed is almost done. They want to complete their "coup" in 2016 but they are playing a long game and they will wait if they have to.

N. L Brisson writes for her own website **The Armchair Observer**. She has a BA degree from SUNY Potsdam and a Master of Education from the University of Arizona at Tucson. She cannot help her liberal leanings; they were an end product of her entire life. She lives in central New York, in a place with very snowy winters.

Please visit my website at http://thearmchairobserver.com/ where I have written about these and other subjects many times.

Or visit my Facebook page at https://www.facebook.com/The-Armchair-Observer-1113923478650446/